Beat Moser

# AROUND THE WORLD IN 30 YEARS

## A Swiss Consul talks

arteMedia

Around the World in 30 Years – a Swiss Consul talks
© 2019 arteMedia, Morschach in Switzerland
www.arte-media.ch
Original title: Von Bomben und Badehosen - Unterhaltsame Beobachtungen eines Schweizer Konsuls

ISBN Book     978-3-905290-89-9
ISBN E-Book   978-3-905290-90-5


Translation:
Douglas Moser, son of author.

Authorship:
Beat Moser wrote many of his experiences himself. Others were recorded and arranged by Stefanie Thoms; naturally as far as possible in keeping with Beat Moser's style.

Thanks:
We should like to thank Beat Moser's son Douglas, who translated the book into English,
and the diligent proof-readers in the family
and Sam Alcordo in Sydney, Australia.

Cover design:
Stefanie Thoms using the graphic designs of © ilolab/Fotolia.

Content responsibility:
The content of this book is based upon the personal experiences and opinions of Beat Moser. His point of view does not reflect the official view of the Swiss Foreign Office (Eidgenössischen Departements für auswärtige Angelegenheiten, EDA).

# Table of contents

Preface ................................................................. 9

Intelligence service ........................................... 11
   Counterintelligence ............................................... 11
   Intelligence gathering ........................................... 14

How the world sees Switzerland ....................... 17
   Miserliness ........................................................... 17
   The whole world is not watching ........................... 18
   The world's most liveable country? ....................... 19
   An approach to saving costs ................................. 20
   The Swiss system – one size fits all? ..................... 21
   Swiss human rights ............................................... 22

From a small village into the big wide world ..... 25
   A tranquil village ................................................. 25
   A blessing ............................................................ 28
   A first taste of the big wide world ........................ 30

Postings ............................................................ 32
   How to become a consular officer ........................ 32
   Manchester (UK, 1975-1976) ............................... 33
   Sydney (Australia, 1976-1980) ............................. 34
   Jakarta (Indonesia, 1979) ..................................... 35
   Sydney again (Australia, 1980) ............................. 39
   Marseille (France, 1980-1983) .............................. 40
   London (UK, 1983-1986) .................................... 43
   Strasbourg (France, 1986-1988) ........................... 44
   Khartoum (Sudan, 1988-1991) ............................ 45
   Melbourne (Australia, 1991-1994) ....................... 48
   Oslo (Norway, 1994-1997) .................................. 49
   Bern (Switzerland, 1997-2001) ............................. 51
   Johannesburg (South Africa, 2001-2003) .............. 53
   Pretoria (South Africa, 2003-2005) ...................... 56
   Moscow (Russia, 2005-2008) ............................... 58
   Leaving your respective new home ....................... 63

## Bribery ............................................................. 67
Bribery methods ................................................. 67
Creative bargaining power .................................. 69
My ethical stance ................................................ 71
No more business with corrupt states ................ 71

## Development aid with side effects ................ 74
Humanitarian aid in Africa ................................. 74
How donations finance arms .............................. 74
Local currency .................................................... 76
What can be donated? ........................................ 77
Why the elites want to maintain the poverty of the masses ................................................................ 80
How consuls engaged on a private basis ........... 82
A different way of dealing with … ..................... 83
What works ........................................................ 85

## How rules of the game differ around the world. 87
How business is conducted around the world .. 87
The power of the media ..................................... 90
World peace ....................................................... 92
Sub-Saharan Africa: sharing ............................... 93
The ball that unites the world ............................ 96

## Looking forward to retirement? ...................... 98
Grumpy old man or active, engaged senior citizen ....... 98
My love of music ............................................... 100
The big blow ..................................................... 102
From shock to gratitude ................................... 103
Victim of circumstances ................................... 107
How thankful we should be ............................. 110
Looking back .................................................... 114

# Preface

Beat Moser loves discussing and debating in a close circle of friends. A lifetime of stories from around the world is listened to attentively. Over thirty years, he lived in a variety of countries: Sudan, Indonesia, Australia, South Africa, Russia and throughout Europe. As a consul, his job was to take care of Swiss citizens and Swiss companies abroad.

Over the years, many of his Swiss friends encouraged Beat to put pen to paper and record his many stories. In 2018, three years after starting this venture, his book is complete. "What a smorgasbord!" exclaim acquaintances. But how else could these stories be packaged. Beat did not experience a couple of exciting years or one fascinating project with a single recurring theme. There are funny stories and insightful experiences as diverse as his postings. Some of the most remarkable occurrences are not permitted on the grounds of privacy/data protection vis-à-vis persons implicated or the actions of the Swiss Foreign Office (Eidgenössisches Departement für auswärtige Angelegenheiten or EDA for short). Not to worry, there are ample anecdotes in the book to reflect on or to chuckle about.

Even though it is not mentioned in the first part of the book, Beat's belief in God played a large role in his life. His faith provided a Christian ethical framework for his conduct throughout his life. When he was diagnosed with cancer after his retirement, his faith in God became more than just an ethical framework. While reading this book, may you hear Beat's stories as though he were telling them himself, with all the energy and conviction, at a table over a glass or two of wine. This book is humorous, thought-provoking, encouraging, disheartening, educational, honest and provocative.

Stefanie Thoms, Publisher arteMedia

# Intelligence service

## Counterintelligence

October 1, 1974 was the start of my new life. Alongside over twenty colleagues who had passed the exams, I was introduced to our new career. One subject in particular attracted everyone's attention. "Ladies and gentlemen, the greatest danger in the consular and diplomatic services is espionage. You know things that others would like to know. An abundance of tricks will be employed in order to obtain this information."

The lion's share of our instruction was focussed on counterintelligence rather than espionage as we were schooled in the methods we would be confronting.
Foreign intelligence services will stop at nothing to obtain information from consular and diplomatic officers in a given country. The favourite 'recruits' are those engaged in an illegal or immoral activity that they would prefer to keep secret. Such individuals are vulnerable and can be pressured. An intelligence service will often set up and hence provoke a situation that the unknowing participant will then regret and wish to keep secret. The individual is then threatened with the disclosure of the event to their respective Head Office or partner, whichever has the most clout. This is the most common way an intelligence service obtains its information, whether it be of a personal or political nature. Too abstract? An example. An officer is invited for dinner. There is plenty of alcohol consumed and laughter but no compromising conversation. A second invitation

soon follows but this time the host is accompanied by attractive women who appear to take pleasure in the consul's company. It is already time to beware. One must never get too close to such individuals. It can be disastrous, especially if photos are taken that could be revealed to a partner. This is how we were schooled. We were to accept a maximum of two invitations from designated people from a variety of nations and never extend a return invitation. We would always greet courteously at events, but would always maintain a safe distance.

In most countries, embassies and consulates are bugged. In some countries, absolutely everything is monitored, including all telephone conversations. This is something that many callers are unaware of and hence careless. They call the office and ask questions regarding the opening of bank accounts or money transfers to Switzerland. The tapping services obviously have a field day with this information and may pass it on to their tax authorities and more.

There are not only informants in embassies. I can imagine that for example a French citizen working for a Swiss bank in Geneva can be recruited to pass on information of account holders to their state in their country of origin. There are millions of people involved in information gathering and counter intelligence around the world. In some embassies, there are more spies than regular personnel; but obviously disguised as visa or cultural officers.

The intelligence agencies of a country's allies provide information, even tip-offs. One hears or reads almost daily that the tip-off of a foreign intelligence agency led to the arrest of X or Y.

The extent of tapping and bugging varies based on the country. It was particularly pronounced in Moscow. We had a Romansch-speaking colleague in the office. As soon as he began talking Romansch on the phone with someone back home, the line would be cut. The reason was that the tapping service had no translator for this rather peculiar and hardly known language (4th national language in Switzerland, spoken by some 50,000 citizens in the country's mountainous South East). We also had to be careful when discarding report drafts. A torn up draft thrown in the waste basket could easily be put back together by the local cleaning lady, who was very likely an employee of the Russian secret service.

It was for this reason that our schooling was focused on counter intelligence. Having said that, intelligence gathering instruction was also required. After all, a key element of our job is to obtain the unofficial opinion in the host country regarding a particular political question. This is mainly the task of senior diplomats.

## Intelligence gathering

So how does a diplomat go about obtaining this unofficial information in their host country?

At the regular cocktail parties and events, we engage with other diplomats, business people, professors, etc. and our host country is the dominant topic. What is behind the latest government decision? Who will benefit most? Is it simply window dressing? How is a decision communicated to the nation's citizens? What photos of an event are likely realistic? What is fake news?

We converse with the leaders of trade associations to gauge the real state of the economy. Such associations generally provide a rather honest picture, somewhat embellished maybe, but rarely completely fabricated.

We talk to government representatives. Depending on the country, facts can be quite manipulated. In some countries, you are informed that all is on track, or that a particular project is running according to plan. However, the trusting individual pays dearly. As a general rule, the higher the degree of press freedom in a given country, the more accurate the official information. The greater the degree of totalitarianism, the less accurately the official information reflects the truth.

We converse with local media representatives, both critical and uncritical. They obviously have very different opinions depending on their political leaning. We talk to people on the street. In such a way, we amass very contradictory opinions of the state of affairs. This then takes time to process. The opinions of the opposition are of particular interest.

Military attachés are primarily concerned with the armed forces. How many aircraft does a nation possess and how many of them are airworthy? How many tanks are operational and where are they stationed? In a country like Russia that is spread over eleven time zones (9,000km from East to West), it is imperative to know where troops and material are stationed. What use would 20,000 tanks stationed in Vladivostok be if a war were to be waged with Western Europe? As with most nations, Russia feels threatened on all fronts. Whether or not a threat really exists, it can help maintaining or increasing a military budget. Furthermore, a foreign enemy – even a fictitious one – can divert citizens' attention from economic or domestic political problems.

Embassy staff are not simply present at events and cocktail parties. We also work. The time spent at evening events is not reimbursed, neither financially nor in time. Whatever time an event finishes, be it midnight or 1am, the office awaits you at the usual time the following morning.

It must be said that you are somewhat proud when you obtain information that no one else has. You possess knowledge that may be sent confidentially to 'Berne' – if the ambassador believes it significant enough – but that you must otherwise keep to yourself. The fact that you must take many stories to the grave is no satisfying prospect.

And what were my duties as a consul? What is the difference between a consular and a diplomatic officer? I spent most of my years in the consular corps. A diplomat spends their time on the political stage. A diplomat conducts and coordinates negotiations in a trade agreement for instance or conveys messages between two governments. A consular officer is responsible for the practical matters concerning Swiss citizens abroad or for a nation's collaboration with Switzerland. This includes the care of some 700,000 Swiss citizens who live abroad, the issuance of visas (e.g. 80,000 per year in Moscow) and the management of local staff and buildings in a given country. A consular officer takes care of Swiss tourists who lose their passports or who get stranded. They also provide contacts for local firms that are interested in collaborating with Swiss firms and vice versa. Another element of the job is maintaining contact with the Swiss community in the host country. There are Swiss clubs all over the world, where Swiss living abroad meet on a regular basis. We were obviously also regular visitors at the many events. The further away the community was from Switzerland, the more intensive the relationship with the homeland. Hence in distant Australia, there are groups of alphorn players, flag throwers and skittle players. There are also Swiss choirs dotted around the globe where traditional songs from back home are sung.

A very important lesson. As a foreigner, I never criticise my host country. I must only observe. I learn to understand my host country. But just because I do not criticise, does not be mean that I approve of everything happening there.

# How the world sees Switzerland

Before I begin writing about my experiences in each of my postings, I should like to clarify one thing – how my years abroad influenced my view of Switzerland.

## Miserliness

I want to get something off my chest today – something that is widespread in Switzerland. Every time I would land back in Switzerland, I would be surrounded by miserable-looking people. What is wrong in the almost perfect Switzerland? Today, I understand the context.

I went to a health resort in the mountains to cure, its location serene and the staff caring. However, I almost only encountered unhappy and troubled people. And what is the reason? I believe that many are miserly, and miserliness hardens the heart and gives rise to loneliness. So how do I come to this conclusion? Most guests take enough food from the breakfast buffet to cover their lunch needs. This way, they can save the twenty francs that lunch in the resort costs. A particularly clever man boasted about his scheme. He would book only bed and breakfast. Every morning, he would fill his tray to the brim with food. After breakfast, he would then stash his hoard of food in the guest fridge and this stockpile would last him until the following morning. How sad. God has given us so much and yet we are not willing to be generous ourselves.

But it was not just miserliness that I encountered, but censoriousness, an addiction to criticise. How the restaurant food would be criticised! It was unbelievable. These people are forgetting how many people around the world do not have enough to live on, and how we lived in Switzerland just one hundred years ago.

## The whole world is not watching

Thirty years living abroad have influenced my way of looking at the world. I lived in completely different societies. And when I returned home for a holiday to see family and friends, I was always surprised by the broadly-held local opinions. One particularly interesting observation was a widely-held preoccupation with how the world views Switzerland. The idea that what was going on domestically was being reported throughout the world. However, decisions on migration or our banking sector for instance go little-noticed abroad. There might be the occasional article on the outcome of a referendum. In Australia, the biggest-selling daily newspapers might feature an average of two articles on Switzerland a year. And our preoccupation with what the world thinks of us? Nothing.

Wherever people are in the world, they have their own problems and do not have capacity or interest in ours'. Take a look through the local television channels. In France, the news is dominated by domestic news followed by a few items of news from the Orient and Africa as a former coloniser in the region.

The same applies for the UK, Germany, the US, Russia and China. One thing all broadcasters have in common, they give their viewers the impression they are well-informed about what is going on around the globe. What a lovely thought.

## The world's most liveable country?

All things considered, Switzerland ranks as one of the world's most liveable countries. On the humour front, however, its ranking does not shine. Its public healthcare tops the ranks, as does its banking system. Other countries are warmer. After Oslo, Switzerland felt sub-tropical. After Khartoum, Melbourne felt arctic on our arrival at the beginning of winter. It always comes down to the comparison you choose.

One very important aspect is the freedom of movement we enjoy in Switzerland. On the whole, our domestic media avoid interference in the private lives of citizens and do not behave like private detectives. This is also a reason that many prominent people chose to holiday in Switzerland. They are able to appear in public, go to restaurant or shop without disturbance.

Compared to international peers, our government bodies are efficient and cost-effective. We can be proud of Switzerland and the Swiss system.

## An approach to saving costs

I recently met with former foreign service (EDA) colleagues. Amongst diverse topics, we talked about the finances of the federal government, expenditure and potential savings. We all agreed on this topic: in the individual departments, cost saving initiatives are scarce. Little notice is taken of parliament's declaration of the need for cost savings.

How do the federal government's cost saving initiatives work? In order to identify the cost savings potential, additional personnel are required at a considerable cost. Once the savings potential is identified, yet more personnel are required for implementation. Once implementation is complete, a department is created to oversee the implemented measures. At the very end of this process, a press release announces that the cost saving target was achieved. Which is not incorrect. It simply ignores the fact that the overall costs have risen for the department in question. This is how it is possible to spend more despite a determined effort to save costs. You need only consult the development of the federal budget to see for yourself.

This approach to saving costs is not the sole reason for the ever-increasing federal government budget; in the age of entitlement, the demands being placed on the government are growing continuously. There needs to be a point of contact, an oversight body or a support organisation for every possible issue. Every request made to the government generates costs. Every newly-passed law triggers a need for an increase in personnel. And this not merely at the federal level, but also at the cantonal and even local government level that are then responsible for the implementation of the new law. We in Switzerland share this burgeoning cost problem with our international peers.

## The Swiss system – one size fits all?

We diplomats are representatives of the Swiss foreign service (EDA) and its – in my opinion – predominantly centre left policy perspective. Sometimes it leans a little more to the centre, sometimes more to the left. We are often invited to discuss the Swiss democratic system with local authorities and members of government in our host country. We explain the ins and outs of our democracy "the only truly viable political system in the world. All countries of the world should adopt the Swiss model." But we are not alone in propagating our system's advantages. Most Western countries are selling the merits of their respective system.

No question that the Swiss democratic system is good, indeed very good. But it can only function in Western societies. I would go as far as to argue that it can only work in Switzerland. Switzerland is a grassroots democratic society. No sooner does a citizen stand out in a crowd, that citizen is hounded off their high horse by the crowd. Many of our neighbours are far more subservient to their governments than the Swiss. A political system that allows citizens to vote for a member of parliament once every four years is sold to them as democratic. Such a system would not work for the Swiss.

Governments function completely depending on the culture of the region and/or country. Gaddafi was forced out of office to make way for a democracy prescribed by the West. At the time, almost no one understood that Libya could not be governed democratically. Libya comprises some fifty tribes, only one of which Gaddafi represented. And he did a rather good job. As arguably the only leader on the African continent, Gaddafi shared the country's oil revenues to provide for free healthcare and education, tax exemption, etc. Influential Libyans even had their medical treatment abroad paid for by the state, including in some hospitals in Berne. The Libyan embassy always paid the private medical invoices, albeit not always punctually.

## Swiss human rights

Back to democracy, the one size fits all form of government for all nations of the world, demonstrating the West's 'understanding' of the rest of the world.

Every time one of our Swiss Federal Councillors visits a peer, the topic of human rights is raised. Each Councillor feels the need to enlighten the leaders of China's 1.4 billion population about the rights of the individual. While a noble cause per se, we risk appearing arrogant or choosing the wrong timing.

During a visit in South Africa, a Federal Councillor addressed women's rights with the country's Justice Minister. Did the Councillor forget that women in Switzerland only won the right to vote in 1971 (only 1990 in the canton of Appenzell Innerrhoden after a Federal Court ruling), and that it took decades to update the applicable laws and regulations. When discussing the birthdate of our democracy, we always refer to 1291 and ignore that until the French Revolution, our land was divided between minority dominators and their subjects. Subject territories included the cantons of Aargau, Thurgau and Vaud. It was only in 1848 that truly democratic structures were born.

It is not only Federal Councillors and Members of Parliament who teach foreign heads of state a lesson, this job is shared by we diplomats. At the behest of Berne, we are to request meetings and lecture them on the benefits of democratic institutions. And this regardless of whether the timing was right to raise our concern. One can imagine how pleasant a job that is. And then when we need something from the authorities, it either takes a lot longer or is not made possible. Examples are abundant. The application for an import licence, their support for the election of a Swiss national to an international committee or for an environmental treaty fall on deaf ears.

One topic that is hardly ever raised as far as I have experienced is the observance of religious freedom. In most countries, religious freedom is guaranteed by law. It is, however, often a very different story in practice. And is such failure to apply the law reprimanded? Hardly. Despite the fact that this renders the lives of Christians and other minorities a torture.

In Switzerland, workers' rights and religious freedom were also fought for. The 1877 Federal Factory Act is just one example. It was a long overdue milestone that, amongst other protective measures for workers, introduced limits on child labour. The Bill was highly contested. If no one stands up for the less well-off, the gap between rich and poor grows and this inequality is not beneficial for either party. New laws are required on a regular basis to rein in the profit-oriented economy and shift the focus to the underprivileged. The world is changing continuously and therewith the balance of power.

# From a small village into the big wide world

## A tranquil village

My story begins in Richigen, the village in the Emmental in which I grew up. It was a village with its peculiarities. I was born into a modest home, as were most children in the village.

I was well known in the village as the local courier who would go from house to house. Once a week, I'd deliver magazines including the "Schweizer Familie", twice a year I'd sell the timetable for public transport. I also sold New Year's cards and distributed bars of soap for the association for the blind. I was hence already familiar with money prior to going to school and was an avid number cruncher on my arrival at school. I had also learnt to read with my older brothers. Needless to say, I was bored at school and had plenty of time for mischief. Together with my buddies, I was responsible for considerable havoc in the village including smashing the village's street lamps with snowballs, unhinging garden gates and getting the odd dog drunk. The latter was highly amusing to us youngsters. Have you ever heard a drunk dog bark? For my teacher, my parents and my brothers such a not sufficiently challenged pupil was a liability.

My father ran a one-man carpentry business and was dependent on the 300-strong local community for work. A rascal like me in the family was not good for business. There was also a second carpenter in the village, alongside two grocery stores, a bakery, a butcher and, of course, the local cheesemaker. In the meantime, all these shops have gone out of business. One needs to travel to the local town of Worb for one's shopping needs today.

The village was my world. At the age of eight, I accompanied my mother to Berne for the first time. And how I marvelled at this metropolis! There were so many people and everyone was running. No one greeted and they were all wearing their Sunday best. Did no one have to work in the city? These well-dressed city-dwellers appeared to simply stroll down the streets and sit in cafes. This was day and night compared to Richigen. Six days a week, people wore their work overalls. Only on Sundays did one dress up in one's finest and took time for a stroll and a relaxing get-together. Saturday evenings entailed the weekly bath in the washing trough, in water heated over the wood fire. An indoor bathroom followed the construction of the sewage system in the village in 1968.

Both my mother and father were active members of the village. Their interaction with their fellow villagers was multifold and included electricity metre reading, informing the community of an impending funeral, the sale of electrical fuses and light bulbs, the replacement of bulbs in street lamps and an egg collection point. Some 3,600 eggs would be collected every week, packed up and taken to the postbus. Each member of the family was engaged in the various jobs to supplement our household income.

To this day, there are some families that shape the village's character; one such family, where the mother was the long-time president of the local women's association. This association played and continues to play a decisive role in helping the less well-off in the village. Or the master painter, who does not merely paint for his customers, but advises them on all things to do with building and construction. He knows the best and most reliable craftsmen and women in Richigen and the surrounding area. This is of particular interest to me as I maintain and rent out the family house that was built in 1904 by my great-grandfather. But many other families are actively engaged. Without the dedicated help of all villagers, we would never have been able to hold the regional wrestling (Schwingen) festival in Richigen. 600 volunteers took care of some 15,000 visitors.

Why am I sharing these details? Everyone knows everyone in a village. One trusts the trustworthy. One knows the generous and the miserly, the friendly and the cranky. There is no hiding. As a youngster, I found this suffocating and needed to leave Richigen for the big wide world. But what did I find there? Richigen on steroids. As in Richigen, there were individuals who influenced life in London, Moscow and Johannesburg. The mix of characters was the same: influential and inconsequential, generous and miserly, intelligent and less clever, open and withdrawn. Moscow is simply 30,000 times larger than Richigen.

## A blessing

But Richigen is also important to me for a completely different reason. I had a handicapped sister. Back then, such a child was not chauffeured daily to a special school or consigned to a home. Ursula, but known in the family and village only as Ursi, lived at home with us and was well-known in the village. To this day, I am very touched by the way the village took on the care of Ursi. She was rarely at home. She would visit neighbours throughout the village daily. They would chat with her, she could watch them while they went about their daily tasks, they would help her with her knitting and always had an eye on her. When it was time for lunch or to return home in the evening, Ursi would be sent on her way. There was no coordination. Everyone just knew. The villagers supported us, my mother in particular, with our fate.

It is incredible how the care of the disabled differs depending on the period and location. During my three years in Moscow, I did not see one single disabled person. Were they living in cellars or were they 'terminated'? In a cold and damp cellar, one would not survive long. In Indonesia on the other hand, there were disabled people on every street corner begging. There was a mafia preying on the sympathy of generous passers-by. Middlemen would collect the disabled from the slums every morning, place them in wealthy districts, each in such a way that the person's disability was highlighted and earned a good income.

The way in which the disabled are cared for in Switzerland these days is exemplary. Their care is all-encompassing, their therapies comprehensive. The disabled are a part of everyday public life. Sometimes, we go a little too far insofar as what is critical to the well-being of the disabled. This in turn raises the cost of their care (as is widespread in our affluent, throwaway society). One issue in this regard troubles me. On the one hand, our society spends copious amounts on operations for the sick and care for the disabled. On the other, it is legal to abort not only disabled but healthy foetuses. Some 10,000 perfectly healthy foetuses are aborted every year in Switzerland. How the women who abort feel in the long run, who often suffer from depression, is not publicised in discussions, only their right to self-determination.

The disabled are not only a blessing for the family into which they are born, but also to broader society. I was privileged to have a disabled sister for over 60 years. She brought our family together more than any other member. Ursi was demonstrative and showed us what pure happiness was really like. There were no ulterior motives. Happiness was happiness, sadness was sadness. We learnt so much from her and through her. I am convinced that all those who knew and stood by Ursi were blessed. Gospel according to Mathew (25:40): "Truly I tell you, whatever you did for one of the least of these brothers and sisters of mine, you did for me."

# A first taste of the big wide world

Having grown up in a little village, the idea of going out to explore the big wide world was particularly attractive to me. My religious education teacher in teachers training college provided the impetus. He was both a church minister and a religious education teacher and we got on very well. He recommended that I travel a few months to Canada or Israel prior to beginning my career as a teacher. And it was he who convinced my parents of the idea.

So a few months later, my plane touched down in Tel Aviv, Israel. We arrived at 4am. All I had was the address of an acquaintance who was living on Kibbutz Dvir, Negev. I wanted to wait on a bench at the airport for dawn before taking a bus south towards the kibbutz. However, then an Israeli approached me and asked what I was doing there. He offered me a lift, put me up for the night before driving me to the kibbutz the following day.

I stayed six months on the kibbutz, picking peaches and then apples. I also worked in the cowshed and the hen house. This was my introduction to modern farming. Chickens were vaccinated, fed antibiotics and were only allowed to sleep two hours a night so they would reach their 1.5 kg slaughter weight within the targeted ten weeks. I was allowed to drive tractors which I thoroughly enjoyed. I spent three months raking straw. And I loved it. Working on these endless fields felt like unadulterated freedom. Our working day began at 4am. Breakfast arrived wherever I was working at 8am. Children from the local Bedouin families who lived in tents nearby would visit me daily and I would share out what I did not manage of the generous meal that I received. Our working day finished at midday. I spent afternoons between my bed and the pool. Shopping was a rather special experience on a kibbutz; one would shop but not pay.

This was the first time I was confronted with multiple cultures. The Jews were returning to Israel from all corners of the globe and this was reflected in their diversity. The boss of the plantations was Moroccan, the boss of the cowshed Dutch and the head of security German. He obviously spoke German and hence we spent plenty of time discussing together. The kibbutz was located between the Gaza Strip and the West Bank, an area in which Arafat's PLO (Palestinian Liberation Organization) was active. They were smuggling weapons and ammunition into the Gaza Strip which required the cover of night. The authorities were obviously aware of this and had soldiers stationed throughout the kibbutz to attempt to prevent this trafficking. The Palestinians have never recognised the state of Israel, indeed, they have made it their goal to destroy it. There were no problems with the Bedouin people. They were grateful for the work (and salaries) on the kibbutz. They continued to enjoy their nomadic life in tents. I once paid them a visit along with a German kibbutz member. In the tent, I was offered a joint and smoked hashish for the first time. I felt very sick very quickly. And in this state, I had to travel back to the kibbutz on the mud guard over the wheel of the tractor. Needless to say, it was also the last time I smoked any such substance. Without this sojourn in Israel, I would most likely never have applied for a career in the foreign service.

# Postings

## How to become a consular officer

Most diplomats have a degree in law, politics or economics. Consular officers on the other hand, have completed their secondary schooling (general qualification for university entrance) or a commercial education. I was the exception as a qualified teacher. Attracted by the big wide world, I applied at the EDA (Swiss Foreign Office) and sat the entrance exam. We were tested in language skills, geography, economics and economic history followed by a personality test. A two-year traineeship followed for the successful applicants. The first three months were taken up with an introductory course in Berne followed by a 20-month placement at a consulate or embassy before returning to Berne for a last month of courses and the final exam.

I am fluent in German, English and French. Depending on the posting, I acquired a basic knowledge of the local language – Norwegian, Arabic and Russian. In most countries around the globe, the Swiss have diplomatic/consular representation where diplomats and consular officers are stationed. Typically, there is an embassy in the capital city and depending on the size and importance of the country, there are consulates in important cities. Embassies with an integrated consular section and consulates officially represent the Swiss government abroad. For both diplomats and consular officers, there is a long career ladder.

# Manchester (UK, 1975-1976)

My first posting in the consular service was Manchester. Here I learnt the consular trade: register Swiss citizens, issue passports and visas, perform the bookkeeping, write flawless official letters, research and provide information in response to concrete queries. An example of such a query: the British education ministry wanted to know what flooring material was used on the playgrounds of Swiss schools and kindergartens.

Particular to this posting were the bomb threats from the IRA (Irish Republican Army). They were fighting to have Northern Ireland returned to Irish sovereignty from British control. According to rumours, four IRA members were in detention in Switzerland and the IRA aimed to obtain their release by means of bomb threats. We were warned by the EDA and received instructions on how to react. We were instructed to check under our vehicles for bombs before every car trip. Press-ups in suit and tie in a rainy climate were not all that popular.

An actual bomb threat to the General Consulate was a terrifying experience. The consulate was located on the 18th floor of the 28-floor Sunley Building. On receipt of the bomb threat, the entire building had to be evacuated. We had to wait an hour in our offices until it was our turn. Obviously, the lifts were out of bounds and hence the evacuation was taking place via the stairwell. We were moving at the pace of the very slowest, our progress held back by the overweight, those on crutches and those with heart problems. We were managing a step every five seconds.

Not exactly reassuring when facing the prospect of an imminent explosion. Needless to say, despite the relatively dull day-to-day job, Manchester remains very vivid in my memory to this day.

## Sydney (Australia, 1976-1980)

Having completed my training, I set off to my first official posting in Sydney. I was delighted to be moving to the distant Australia. My parents were less ecstatic. Rather horrified. Back in those days, Australia was a lot further away than it is today in terms of travel time and relative cost.

Australia attracted a wide variety of Swiss nationals. There were the stranded, adventurers, dropouts, former bankers who bought farms and raised cattle, proponents of self-sufficient farming and those who wanted none other than to spend their life on a surfboard.

I will never forget this one call. A Swiss citizen phoned from northern Australia, some 2,000km north of Sydney. He informed me that he was about to commit suicide and simply wanted the Consulate General to know. He then abruptly hung up. What was I to do? I immediately notified the local police. Three months later, I received a visit from the gentleman. He came to our office to thank me for the support. He had been treated in a psychiatric clinic and was on his way to visit his family in Switzerland.

Alongside my consular duties, I was tasked with producing Swiss programs for "Ethnic Radio Australia", a radio channel that broadcast news and entertainment programs for the country's immigrant communities. Seven hours a week were allocated to the German-speaking community, 30 minutes of which was assigned to the Swiss. This proved terrific relief from the rather administrative nature of my 'day job'. The programs were always live. Lights began flashing followed by a voice "five, four, three, two, one, go…". The programs had obviously to be well-prepared. I was given free rein as to the content. I prepared a summary of the week's Swiss news. I also interviewed numerous celebrities including the Swiss author, Peter Bichsel, who was touring Australian universities for readings to their German language students.

The difference in mentalities between the Australians and the Swiss on the environment was dramatic. My suburban neighbour would return home for lunch and would leave the engine of his V8 running for the 30 minutes to keep his car cool. Back in Switzerland, we recycled everything down to aluminium yoghurt tub lids.

## Jakarta (Indonesia, 1979)

My four-month posting from August to December 1979 in Indonesia provided the most challenging consular situations of my career.

Let us begin with the death of a Swiss citizen on a remote island in South East Asia. It is the duty of consulates and embassies to inform the foreign office in Berne of accidents and deaths involving Swiss nationals abroad. The foreign office then informs the relatives via the police, the local authority or the parish office.

I received the following news from the authorities in Papua New Guinea: "We have the human remains of a Swiss citizen in our morgue which has no refrigeration capacity. While on a caving tour with fellow students, he was hit by unexpected high water while crossing a river and drowned. It took his companions a few days to organise a helicopter to have his body transported to Port Moresby." The embassy in Jakarta finally received this information. The victim's family in Switzerland had to be informed.

The authorities in Papua New Guinea also wanted to know what the family wanted to do with the victim's remains. Communication back in the day was not quite as straightforward as it is today and further exacerbated by the 10-hour time difference. Step one was a telex to the foreign office in Berne.

A day later we received the reply: "The body should be flown to Switzerland." The answer from Port Moresby: "No airline willing to transport the corpse due to the extent of decomposition." This was communicated to Berne with the request for alternative instructions. The following day came the reply: "Please have the corpse shipped to Switzerland" which we telexed to Port Moresby. We received the answer the same day: "No ship willing to transport corpse." This message was forwarded to the relatives. Their reply was to have him cremated which we forwarded to Port Moresby. Their reply followed shortly: "There is no crematorium in Papua New Guinea. The closest crematorium is located in Brisbane, Australia." Messaged to Switzerland. Reply: "Have the body cremated in Brisbane."

Port Moresby's prompt reply: "No ship nor airline will transport the corpse due to the advanced stage of decomposition. Please send us definitive instructions as the decaying corpse can no longer be kept in our non-refrigerated morgue." At this, I picked up the telephone and called the responsible authority in Port Moresby. I asked innocently if a crematorium was actually necessary to cremate a body. An hour later I received the good news: "cremation possible in Papua New Guinea" and forwarded it to Switzerland. The OK from Berne followed, as well as relief and thanksgiving.

By chance, a year later, I was given details of the cremation ceremony. The local Hindus' ceremony involved music, dance, flowers and prayer. The victim's relatives could not have wished for a more beautiful farewell.

And now to a sad chapter in this book; the plight of the Vietnamese refugees. Far more difficult than the tragic incident described above was my work with these refugees. They had run ashore on multiple Indonesian islands. Indonesia is made up of some 17,500 islands. And they had arrived in their thousands. This was Vietnam's crème de la crème.

Why were the Vietnamese fleeing Vietnam? The communist North invaded the capitalist South. The educated upper-class were either killed or placed in re-education camps. A few thousand-dollar ransom payment would buy a 'prisoner' the right to flee camp and country aboard a refugee boat. With a bare minimum of personal effects, they were travelling on unsafe boats, a phenomenon we are all too familiar with today in the Mediterranean.

On their arrival, they applied for asylum in multiple Western countries. On behalf of Switzerland, I received many thousand applications. The communication between Jakarta and Berne was arduous. There was no email back in the day. Phone calls were far too expensive and in any case the administration insisted on having everything in writing. Hence, all communication was conducted via telex. For our younger readers: the telex system functions similar to a telephone network but for text-based messages as opposed to spoken communication. Instead of a telephone, there was a teleprinter – a sort of typewriter – that incorporated a 5-hole paper-tape punch and reader. Once the paper tape was prepared, the message could be transmitted to the recipient. In this manner, we would transmit the asylum applications to Switzerland.

And when we finally received the reply from Berne, many of the refugees had already been granted refugee status in other countries. Most wanted to go to the US. Only those with relatives or friends in Switzerland were interested in our country.

Communication with the refugee camps was sub optimal. I was thus forced to travel to the refugees – who were distributed throughout the islands – in person. I was on the go in planes and boats – an old fishing boat because the helicopter was out of order

– to the northern most islands of Indonesia. Once, a helpful UNHCR commissioner provided me with a translator.

My questioning was met with horrific tales. On their boat journeys, the refugees were held up and robbed multiple times. The pirates were most interested in cash and jewellery. Women's fingers were simply cut off to remove rings. Women and children were raped by the pirates. Anyone who did not cooperate would be thrown overboard. The vast majority were traumatised. All the same, I was forced to inflict each interrogation to be able to complete the forms for Berne. My very worst moment was receiving the specified 'number' of refugees that would be receiving asylum in Switzerland from Berne. Those who had not made the list were abandoned. It was my duty to inform each unsuccessful applicant personally. Their eyes divulged their pain. It was almost unbearable. There were many sleepless nights. After all, consular officers are also human.

## Sydney again (Australia, 1980)

After my four-month intermezzo in Jakarta, I was back in Australia. When my oldest brother brought the news that my father was suffering from cancer in February 1980, the distance between Australia and my Swiss home became all the more apparent. To be so far from a dying father was very tough. I flew to Switzerland in March for five weeks to be with my family and share this burden, staying with my brothers or parents as always.

Prior to my departure, I had received a book from the local church minister in Engadine (Sydney). The book by Elisabeth Kübler Ross dealt with how to go about with the terminally ill. It proved a great help when talking with my father. We unfortunately never spoke directly about his imminent passing. I felt he did not want to discuss it. We exchanged banalities. I only cried when I was no longer in his presence. We all did it; my mother, my brothers.

But then came the final farewell. A farewell knowing that I would not see him alive again. Words fail me. He died in July. A phone call brought an end to the waiting. But it was a shock all the same. Every death is accompanied by dismay, even if one actually wishes the death that will relieve someone of their pain. I did not attend his funeral, something I regret to this day. My move to Marseille was scheduled for the following month and it felt like too much – I was in the midst of planning a move half way around the world.

## Marseille (France, 1980-1983)

In Manchester, we endured multiple bomb threats but never actually saw a bomb. It was a different story in Marseille. There were no threats in Marseille. My colleague made a disturbing discovery one morning. He was the first to arrive and discovered a package in front of the door of our 2$^{nd}$ floor office. There was a timed detonator on the outside as well as a battery and otherwise looked like a bomb. He ran out of the building to the restaurant next door screaming "une bombe". The restaurant owner called the police. It was indeed a bomb, packed into a plastic bag and furnished with a detonator. According to rumours, French separatists trying to obtain the freedom of detained colleagues were responsible. But we were never informed. The battery had been too weak to detonate the bomb. It would otherwise have already have exploded. We had to learn how to deal with never knowing if and when you might be blown up.

Marseille was in many ways an interesting posting for consular officers. I can not count how many tourists appeared in the waiting room of our consulate general in their bathing suits having been robbed of all other belongings. They had taken only their bathers, a towel and car keys to the beach. They'd left all other valuables in the safety of their car. And that was now gone.

We had an excellent agreement with the French (SNCF) and Swiss (SBB) railways. In the consulate, we could issue railway tickets (one-way Marseille – Geneva and one-way Geneva – place of residence). The 'stranded' would also receive a little pocket money and a deposit slip. And for those who had no clothes, they could serve themselves from the piles of clothing in our lost and found that were deposited by the local police and authorities on a daily basis throughout the tourist season. From time to time, it got rather entertaining watching these stricken people trying on the clothes on offer, performing a sort of fashion show.

A large part of our work was consumed with the many delinquents from Switzerland who had become stranded in the South and were handed over by the local police. They were threatened with criminal prosecution back home and headed south to go into hiding, join the Foreign Legion or simply start a new life. When things did not work out and these Swiss nationals were brought to the consulate, they would 'only' be handed a train ticket from Marseille to Geneva. On their arrival at the border, they would be taken into custody by the Swiss authorities. Naturally, not all completed their trip home but would disembark before their arrival in Geneva. But at some point, their exodus would come to an end. Upon their third or fourth visit to the consulate penniless, we would look into an alternative solution to get them back to Switzerland.

Another particularity to our job in Marseille was the number of mentally ill who believed all would be better down South. One case involved a patient at a psychiatric institution in Switzerland. He was working on the integrated farm and did not like it. So, one day, he simply 'borrowed' a car that had a key in the ignition and drove until the car ran out of petrol. He almost managed to the south coast of France. He finally ended up being handed over by the local police to us – it was a Sunday. I remember it well. He stank. And I had to drive him to a medical examiner and then to a psychiatric clinic. My car stank for weeks.

A further interesting fact that I came across in Marseille was the collaboration with the Swiss Maritime Navigation Office in Basel. Switzerland is landlocked but some 25 ocean-going vessels operated under the Swiss flag (today there are approximately 50). Our job at the consulate was to board all Swiss flag flying ships that docked in Marseille – about every two weeks – and check and validate all the ship's paperwork (maritime licenses, certificates, etc.), check the teams' documents, etc. Once complete, we would often be invited by the captain for a meal. Most of the chefs were Italian and the food was delicious. In the absence of good food, there would most likely have been considerably more infighting on those ships. Of paramount importance was a good relationship with the port authorities. In the event of war, it was critical that Switzerland would be able to maintain supplies from abroad via these ports. Maintaining this relationship was one of the Consul General's most important duties.

I was never bored in Marseille and found the time to enjoy the climate. I would often head to a beach or go walking in the Calanques with a friend.

## London (UK, 1983-1986)

I have wiped my time in London from my memory. I was so fortunate to have the chance to live in such an interesting city – and yet I did not live it. My life was abound with personal problems, including the illness and death of my mother to whom I was very close, and I was in search of a meaningful future. I went looking in the wrong place, the alternative space. The more I found, the emptier I felt. But I did not want to admit it. One blessing to come out of this period: it became clear to me that there was no alternative to a belief in the Almighty.

Otherwise, the job in London was varied. Of particular interest was to be well informed of all the latest diplomatic exchange between Switzerland and the United Kingdom.

## Strasbourg (France, 1986-1988)

In Strasbourg, I assumed the role of Head of Chancellery – head of the consular division – for the first time.

It was May 1986, the height of asparagus season. At every event, asparagus was on the menu. I ate until I finally reached the point of saturation.

Many interesting and well-known people came to Strasbourg for readings, including Peter Bichsel and Mousse Boulanger. I will always remember a visit from Friedrich Dürrenmatt in whose honour I organised a dinner. One could already see signs of his illness but his personality outshone it all.

One of the various tasks of a consul is visiting prisoners. Our role is to confirm that the minimum standards of hygiene, board and lodging are complied with in addition to access to legal representation. The vast majority of prisoners that I visited during my career were in and around Strasbourg. Almost all had been caught smuggling drugs (buying in Holland and transporting them via Belgium and France to Switzerland).

The vehicle they were traveling with would be automatically impounded and then sold at auction. Since for many dealers, their means of transport was their most important asset, I would be asked to provide them with the timing of the auction. Their accomplices could then bid at the auction and secure the vehicle's return to its previous owner. The drug addicts amongst the prisoners did not suffer the withdrawal symptoms for too long and would soon settle for the methadone that the prison's doctor would prescribe. Those who did not, would soon gain access to the drug-trafficking within the prison. One prisoner would write letters for his prison mates. He was in demand as many of the prisoners were unable to put pen to paper. He would tell me about the declarations of love he would write for them.

It was in Strasbourg that my car with diplomatic number plates was stolen for a bank robbery, a first in my career. It was used as a getaway car. With the diplomatic plates, the car was able to be parked 'illegally' right in front of the bank. The car was stolen in broad daylight from in front of the consulate where policer officers were on guard.

## Khartoum (Sudan, 1988-1991)

There is plenty to recount from my time in Sudan. This posting features in multiple chapters later in the book. Khartoum had a greater impact on me than any other posting. There were plenty of hardship. In one of Africa's poorest countries, a raging civil war killed some 300,000 people per year. The Northerners of Arabic origin were fighting the African Southerners. This war was exacerbated by fighting between tribes. Every year there were peace negotiations, every year the wars continued. At the time, media coverage of Sudan back in Switzerland was practically non-existent. Over 90% of Swiss residents could not locate Khartoum on a map.

It was quite thrilling to live in a region where almost nothing functioned, where one could barely obtain basic foodstuffs, diesel or petrol. We rarely had electricity. During the World Cup in 1990, we had electricity for the duration of each match. There would have been massive protests had the government not managed that. In shops and at markets, there was hardly anything on sale. No apples, no milk, no butter. There were usually five kinds of vegetable. There was meat, but we never bought it. It would be hanging throughout the day in high temperatures - Khartoum is the world's hottest capital city – and would be hardly visible behind the swarms of flies having a feast. We imported almost everything with Lufthansa Catering and stowed it in three freezers and two fridges. Due to the sporadic electricity supply, we needed generators. They were incredibly loud. Our local personnel could not relate to our needs. Our generators were never switched on when we were away. On our return from a holiday, everything had gone off in temperatures that could climb above 50c in the shade. But we learned from these experiences and would transport our fridges and freezers to friends during absences. This also meant that our living room was often populated with the fridges and freezers of friends and colleagues.

There were 15 minutes of news in English per day on the local single television station. All other programs were in Arabic, comprising mainly of Egyptian soaps. The news brought the same message every day: how the situation was improving for the country and its people. We were lucky to have a shortwave radio to be able to listen to the BBC World Service.

Why did we have an embassy in Sudan at all? We could not buy anything from the nation, nor could we sell anything. We were simply there to alleviate the poverty. We 'invested' a lot of money and even more patience but our achievements were all but trivial. And we were far from the only player in the humanitarian sector. There were hundreds of aid organisations and missionaries. They were all required to import hard currency and exchange it to local currency at a bank. I deal in detail with this topic – a favourite of mine – in a later chapter entitled "Development aid with side effects".

At the Swiss Embassy, we were three "Chawadjas" (as white foreigners were called) and several Sudanese and Eritrean employees. Some would cheat us and our system, taking advantage of the fact that we did not understand Arabic. Visas would be sold (something we could prove only with great difficulty), official cars would be used for private purposes as well as for people and material transport. When embassy cars needed diesel, Abdullah would be on the go or up to five hours to fill the car's fuel tank. We can only imagine what he got up to with these cars with diplomatic number plates. Needless to say, Abdullah earned well.

Our security detail was rather special. The military provided a soldier for each of our buildings (embassy, ambassador's residence and two consular officer residences). In addition, we hired a private security company that provided a guard. However, since they were paid so little, they all had two jobs. They would work during the day and sleep at night. All our guards slept, with their weapon as a pillow.

In Sudan I became acquainted with the 'cycle' that all newcomers face on their arrival in a poor African country: the first year, one is full of enthusiasm and desperate to help and alleviate the suffering. All instruments on hand are deployed. The second year, frustration boils over and one is irate that almost nothing works. Either the authorities are blocking your efforts or your African employees lack the entrepreneurial spirit to carry projects forward. Without this capacity for a proactive approach that we take for granted, hardly a venture goes without breakages and waste. In the third year, one comes to the realization that it is not an issue of individual failings, but the entire system is at fault. One stops engaging as it is anyway of no use. One turns to directly helping small ventures where one knows that assistance bears fruit.

## Melbourne (Australia, 1991-1994)

My job was not particularly inspiring. I headed both the consular and trade divisions. I was also responsible for the four pages dedicated to Australia in the quarterly "Swiss Review" magazine that is distributed to all Swiss nationals living outside their home country.

On the other hand, the country was inspiring. I loved Australia's vast expanses. We travelled by car half way around the continent with family and friends. For hours on end, no change in scenery, no curve in the road. We would hardly ever see a living kangaroo, only their lifeless corpses on the side of the road. They would be run over by road trains, trucks with up to four trailers, essentially a freight train on the road. The trucks are mounted with bull bars (locally know as roo (kangaroo) bars) that clear everything in their path.

A visit to a prison was particularly impressive. A Swiss traveller entered Australia smuggling drugs. He had wanted to finance his stay in Australia with the proceeds. He flew via Singapore into Melbourne with a counterfeit passport and was caught. I had to travel 300km north of Melbourne to visit him. The prison was made up of small houses spread over a huge site with swimming pools and tennis courts. Upon my departure, I spoke with a supervisor and suggested that the institution resembled more of a holiday camp than a prison. His reply: "Way too bloody good for those bastards". Our countryman was in luck that he was not serving time somewhere in Asia.

## Oslo (Norway, 1994-1997)

Nor was my job in Oslo inspiring. An aspect of my job there that was special was the collaboration with the Swiss colony. With colony I mean all the Swiss nationals who live in a foreign country and for whom the consulate is responsible. The Swiss community was made up mainly of women who had married Norwegians. How had this come about? There were very few university places in Norway and hence scores of those wanting to study had to head abroad. Many young Norwegians studied at Zurich's ETH and found themselves a Swiss girlfriend. Many relationships translated into marriages and often couples headed north to Norway.

Norwegians are reserved. I would often invite such couples to our home (my wife is an excellent cook and host). The Swiss wives would chat but their Norwegian husbands would hardly utter a word, drinking in silence. But they wouldn't want to leave either. Eleven o'clock would come and go and there was hardly more conversation than "Skol" (Norwegian for cheers). This would go on until midnight. Enlightenment came after about a year. In Norway, it was polite to stay at least until midnight. Leaving earlier implied the hosts had done a bad job.

One Saturday, I received a phone call from the police in far northern Norway. There was a Swiss citizen with neither papers nor money, claiming it had been stolen. They sent him to Oslo and I put him up in a hotel on Sunday night before I could begin with the clarification and administrative process to organise his return to Switzerland. What he had obviously omitted, is that he had been at a drug rehabilitation camp in the far north of the country and had run away. At such camps, clients are expected to find their way back to normal life. They were to procure their own food, fishing or hunting. His return to Switzerland was authorised and was taken into custody by the police on arrival. Embassy and consular staff are duty-bound to assist all Swiss citizens, be they poor or wealthy, tourist or criminal. Only dangerous criminals require an escort on their return to Switzerland and police agencies collaborate to ensure effective passage.

## Bern (Switzerland, 1997-2001)

Unexpectedly, I received the request from headquarters to return to Berne. I was not thrilled at the prospect but obliged nonetheless.

However, in Berne, I was given very interesting assignments. One of my tasks was the coordination of all openings and closures of embassies and consulates globally. There was plenty of demand for intervention on this front in the ex-Soviet Union and ex-Yugoslavia. All of a sudden, instead of two states, there were 20. In the most important capital cities, embassies had to be established. This was no simple task. Authorisation was required to establish an embassy, an appropriate building had to be found, a purchase or rental agreement signed, renovation and security works carried out, the post required staffing, a residence found and renovated for the mission head (each incorporating Berne's security standards), short wave radio connectivity and once again personnel. But personnel were always available. Foreign office staff were almost always open to a new challenge in a new location. It was very rare to have to 'send' someone against their will.

The expansion of the embassy network was to be more or less cost neutral and hence it was to be accompanied by the closure of consulates. Two consulates that I'd worked were included in the reorganisation; Melbourne (to be covered by general consulate in Sydney) and Manchester (to be covered by general consulate in Edinburgh). Naturally, the closures did not sit well with the local Swiss communities and delegations would arrive in Berne to dispute the decisions.

I was also a member of the management team for an IT project. It concerned the then approximately 650,000 Swiss nationals living abroad at the time. Their combined data was to be uploaded into a central database in Berne that all consular and diplomatic missions around the globe would have access to. A unique project. It had never been done before; neither amongst the residents' registration offices (the integration of local authorities and cantons) nor abroad. I was given the task of overseeing the old-age insurance system (contributors and retirees), in collaboration with department of finance, department of home affairs and the foreign office (EDA). We were a group of five: two from Geneva, one from London and two from Berne. Instead of the usual full-day meetings held in offices, we would meet on the lake of Geneva, take the three lakes tour, hold a meeting in Yverdon-les-Bains and spend our lunch break in the thermal baths, or we'd meet in a restaurant with a beautiful view. We all paid our additional costs ourselves (we received a daily allowance of 25 Swiss francs each). I was of course considered a tourist at headquarters. But the work was always done, and the project was successfully completed within four years. The test phase was conducted in Montreal and hence I finally set foot on American soil, the only continent I had never been posted to.

## Johannesburg (South Africa, 2001-2003)

Africa's most southern country is a land of extremes. South Africa's climate is wonderful, rarely hot, rarely cold. The wildlife is exquisite. We spent literally weeks in the safari parks, some of which were huge. Kruger National Park is some 300km long. This is like driving from Geneva to St. Gallen and seeing hundreds of wild animals along the whole route: gnus, elephants, giraffes, buffalo, lions, cheetahs and rhinos. Our most memorable experience was in a camp on the border to Botswana. There were no fences. We were living together with wild animals, large and small. The day began at 4am. We piled into an open top Land Rover where we spent four hours on safari. At 8am, we returned to the camp for breakfast and rested for a few hours. At 4pm, we were back on the go until 8pm. Animals are most active at dawn and dusk. What we witnessed during those eight hours each day in the open 4x4s was overwhelming. Another excursion took us to an elephant sanctuary. Every member of the group was allocated an elephant for the day. An elephant is a wonderful and surprisingly sensitive animal. If I could ever choose a special pet, I would choose an elephant.

We would return from a safari excursion to the big city and the daily grind. We loved our welcome home from our two German shepherds who would bark with excitement, their tails wagging wildly. We were always happy to find them alive and well. All too often dogs would be fed poisoned meat by burglars. A house-owner would return to a dead or dying dog (shivering and foaming at the mouth). But this would be just the start of your welcome. The house would be practically empty. Anything that remained would be broken. And all this would happen despite all possible security measures: a security company, a two-metre wall around the property on top of which stood a 40cm high 8,000-watt electric fence, infrared motion detector, floodlights, barred windows and doors, four cameras around the house and an alarm system. Essentially all the security one can buy. And despite this, there was a burglary or attempted burglary once a week in our row of houses that backed onto a public path along a river. This was not good for one's nerves. Many of our neighbours had guns and at night would shoot at anything that moved down by the river.

We had only one break-in and a rather remarkable one at that. For security reasons, we had all the trees at the bottom of our large garden cut down to prevent burglars from simply getting over the wall via the trees' branches. We employed a gardener to fell the trees. At the time, we noticed that the gardener's employees got on well with our dogs and were feeding them. This is unusual in Africa whose inhabitants are not fond of dogs. We found out the reason soon after they had finished their gardening job. The gardeners returned to our property and the dogs did not bark. But they did not climb over the wall to get into the garden, but dug a tunnel under it. Luckily for us, they were unaware of the infrared motion detectors in the garden that set off the alarm and ignited the floodlights. The burglars left our property in a hurry, leaving behind their excavation tools.

These problems were not limited to one's home; they were ever-present on the roads. At every red light, one had to try to avoid finding a gun aimed at one's head. We had bullet-proof glass fitted to our cars and were connected via satellite with a security company. This obviously helped the nerves. But our activities were not limited to our house and the road where we could install a degree of security. My wife went to the local bank to withdraw money at the teller when she was threatened by an African man armed with a pistol. The bank's guard intervened. And what happened? The guard was shot dead and the bank robber walked calmly out of the bank and into the crowd.

It is tragic that all burglars and thieves are Africans. We came to South Africa with high hopes that after the end of apartheid, the election of an African president (Nelson Mandela) and a majority African parliament, that relations would normalise. But this was not the case. Whites generally feared Africans and their suburbs were no-go zones. Africans did not trust the whites. Apartheid still existed in day-to-day life. The situation in Zimbabwe exacerbated the security situation in South Africa. Hundreds of thousands of Zimbabweans fled the prospect of starvation back home. Mugabe, the country's ruler, lived the lap of luxury leaving absolutely nothing to the people. In South Africa, these northern neighbours lived illegally and would be incarcerated on discovery. For Zimbabweans, burglary was a win-win situation: if a burglary was successful, they could sell the stolen goods and would have a little money; if they were caught, they would be imprisoned and fed.

The lack of security in Johannesburg was our greatest concern. The setting was perfect, living in a beautiful and spacious house with pool, adjacent to a river and surrounded by 40-metre high trees. An ideal world in a photo. And yet, reality was so completely different. Anyone who has spent a few years in South Africa could write a book on such episodes.

## Pretoria (South Africa, 2003-2005)

I was initially stationed at the General Consulate in Johannesburg. Following its closure, I moved to the embassy in Pretoria.

My last two postings in South Africa and Russia, prior to my retirement, were exclusively devoted to trade. My mission was to provide all the necessary contacts and information to Swiss companies interested in doing business in the respective country.

The new government in South Africa had undertaken many measures for those who had been underprivileged under the previous regime. Entitled "Black Empowerment", a new legislative decree was passed in 2004 allowing the African population the right to ownership of companies. They received interest-free loans for up to 99% of the necessary capital. From one day to the other, there were many new company owners, but not all in possession of the necessary know-how. Furthermore, since very little private funds were required, the commitment was often limited. It works the same way wherever you go in the world. The decisions of large firms' top management can differ significantly depending on whether or not they have their own funds invested in the company. They manage the company from bonus round to bonus round. Western companies' South African counterparts were exchanged overnight. One needed to get to know these new local decision-makers to stay in business with them. Considerably more time was needed to close a deal.

The longer I lived in Southern Africa, the less I understood the local people. On the one hand, there was a harmony between them that I had never seen elsewhere in the world. This was very apparent in singing. More on this topic later.

On the other hand, the African continent is dominated by a gaping polarity. We often have a picture of Africans living in small mud huts in the countryside. However, most people live in rapidly-growing cities. There are architecturally-impressive, top modern high-rise buildings that stand in stark contrast to the slums on the outskirts of the cities that house millions of people.

The 40,000 murders and 70,000 rapes of minors annually was horrifying (estimated figures for South Africa during my time in the country. The official statistics were lower based only on reported cases).

There was a wide-spread belief amongst African men that Aids could be cured through sexual intercourse with a healthy (Non-HIV positive) person. Virgins, including infants, would be raped most often by relatives – fathers, grandfathers, uncles, etc. Most infants died as a consequence. Simply incomprehensible.

Africans are skilled craftsmen. With the simplest of tools, they manage the most exquisite of carvings. We would admire the wooden animal figures sold along the side of the road and at local markets. Watching their carving skills live was truly splendid.

But a lot simply did not work. Whether or not they possessed a watch, they were never punctual. And we are not talking about five or ten minutes late, it would be hours, days, weeks or even months. They would very rarely adhere to deadlines. Even when it was in their interest. One had to ask oneself if Swiss have a built-in clock and Africans not.

So much is extraordinary on the African continent. It is impressive to experience how African Christians live their faith, so joyfully, naturally and persuasive.

## Moscow (Russia, 2005-2008)

Moscow was not my dream posting at the outset. Prior to my departure for Moscow, I had to visit numerous government agencies and chambers of commerce to get informed. Wherever I went, I feigned enthusiasm for the upcoming role. But how could I be looking forward to the posting after decades of brainwashing? We had been trained to fear the evil communist countries to the East, with Russia leading the pack.

We arrived and were met by a friendly colleague who brought us to our hotel. This was a welcome break from the scowls we were greeted with at immigration and customs - Russians are renowned for their scowling. We were tempted to jump on the same plane back to Zurich. The hotel staff were not much friendlier. We were given the impression that we were disturbing their inactivity. After unpacking our cases, we headed to the hotel restaurant for a bite to eat. The following morning, I was picked up from the hotel and accompanied on and introduced to the metro to the embassy. The journey there went well. Needless to say, the return journey alone proved a little more challenging with all signage in Cyrillic script. In my three years in Moscow, I survived all my travel on the metro and arrived at my destination most of the time. Since my schedule forced me to travel at peak travel times, I became all too aware of the disadvantages of being small. We were at the end of a line and hence boarding was not an issue. At every station, new commuters joined and I would be pushed to the middle of the carriage. Not only would I have fellow commuters' packages in my face and would be overwhelmed by the scents of vodka and garlic, but I had to fight my way to the doors to be able to alight at my station. I developed a strategy over time. Speaking Bern Deutsch worked rather well. I would say "Uf d'Site bitte!". My fellow Russian commuters would take a step back to examine the speaker of this strange language that they did not understand. This was the way I managed to get to the door in time to exit at my stop.

In complete contrast to the Russians on the street, my colleagues at the embassy were all very polite. The approximately 50 Russians employed at the embassy were appreciative of their privileged position. I assume that several of them were living on two salaries: the Swiss one and one from the FSB, the successor of the KGB, Russia's infamous secret service.

My role as head of the trade desk was extremely interesting. Russia had major catching up to do on the machinery, material and know-how fronts. We were inundated with enquiries. And many companies in Switzerland wanted to sell their goods to Russia. Ideal basis for a business relationship.

In Moscow, there was money and combined with Russians' generosity meant we had considerable freedom. When we moved into new offices and were planning an opening ceremony, we quickly found a sponsor to fly over a Swiss folklore ensemble. How were we going to locate such a group? Not a problem for someone who'd been brought up in a village like myself. I called a friend in Richigen and asked: "do you know of an ensemble that would be willing to come to Moscow to play?". "Of course, I do" came the answer. Only one further phone call was required to have the traditional accordion ensemble "Campagna" come to Moscow. They ended up coming three times to Moscow. They were not paid for their performances, only their flights, board and lodging. Their music had warmed the hearts of hundreds if not thousands of Russians.

In Russia, business rarely takes place in offices. Russians love events, cocktails, where you can meet an array of local and international personalities. Only the best is good enough for your wife, your friends or your guests in Russia. A piece of meat, two potatoes and a couple of peas would be an insult to a Russian. On any table, there must be at least double the amount that can be eaten. This is not wasteful, simply good hospitality. And we must not forget that the Russians like the Swiss.

Something I must say about all the cultures with which I have had the privilege to encounter: one criticises what one does not know. The longer one lives in a country, the better one gets to know and understand the people and their peculiarities. This is particularly challenging in Russia due to the country's size – double the size of America with half the population. It is a multi-ethnic state with a considerable Muslim population. There are numerous conflict areas, in the Northern Caucasus in particular. In the big cities, the security apparatus is enormous. There was talk of some 300,000 police and security officials in Moscow alone. As I was leaving South Africa for Russia, I was asked by so many if I was not scared of living in Russia. This was a stance I had to refute. Every person was at risk in South Africa; in Russia there were mainly contract killings. And relatively few of them. I felt safe on the streets, obviously helped by the presence of 300,000 security personnel. What was dangerous, was the driving style of road users. One was often grateful to have arrived safely at a destination.

There was an organisation for wealthy Russians whose goal it was to provide their clientele with any object at any time. We attended an event staged by the organisation. The organisation's boss showed the building's underground garage. There were some 30 Bentleys, 10 Rolls-Royces, six Aston Martins, 10 Ferraris, Lamborghinis, to mention but a few. And every one of these cars was available for immediate sale, of course, against cash payment. There was also an enormous jewellery shop open around the clock, 365 days a year, for the organisation's members.

I required a translator for my tasks in Russia. In earlier postings, I had almost always managed with English and French. However, in Russia, only Russian worked. I once suggested to a group of business people that they might want to learn English to ease their access to world markets. Their prompt answer: "You have to learn Russian. We are a world power."

The cold left a lasting impression on me. The closest metro station to our apartment block (which comprised 555 of them) was a 20 minute-walk away. In winter, temperatures sunk to minus 37 degrees Celsius which was often exacerbated by wind. It was tough. In addition to multiple layers of clothing, I would smear Vaseline on my face. One could only use pure fat. Alternative water-based cremes would freeze on your skin with the obvious consequences.

I would encounter plenty of people on my way to the Jugo-Sabatnaya metro station every morning. It was a different story in the evening or at night. There would be lifeless bodies, vodka bottle in hand, lying on park benches or on the ground. One could not tell if some were still alive. But in the morning, everything was back to normal again. I never found out what happened to these people. As cynical as it sounds, it may have been simpler for the city authorities to let these inhabitants freeze to death.

Moscow turned out to be one of the most interesting postings of my career. I would have preferred it a little warmer. But the time to bid Russia farewell came.

I was given the choice between another posting abroad or early retirement. A transfer would have entailed the usual change of education system for children, building a new professional network again, etc. I chose early retirement. We packed our Volvo, drove to St. Petersburg, took the ferry to Lübeck from where we drove the length of Germany to Zurich.

## Leaving your respective new home

I want to address the inner turmoil, anguish and uncertainty that the regular transfers would trigger. Leaving a posting was much more difficult than starting in the new location. I will explain with an anecdote. My posting in Johannesburg came to an unexpected end when the consulate general in the city was closed in November 2003. The consular and trade departments were integrated into the embassy in Pretoria.

I was initially informed by headquarters in Berne that I would not be going to Pretoria. I had been earmarked for the post of Counsellor at the embassy in Kinshasa, Democratic Republic of Congo. But this transfer did not materialise. Then it was Addis Ababa. We were rather happy at this prospect. Ethiopia was a neighbour of Sudan where we'd already lived. The capital is located 2,300 metres above sea level which implied a moderate climate. Housing the African Union's headquarters meant there was a good deal going on. We spent plenty of time at a holiday trade fair in Johannesburg looking into stabile 4x4s with rooftop tents. We would again buy a Toyota Landcruiser African version with a roof top tent that would allow us to camp out in the wilderness. We were completely sold on this posting.

Then came the next phone call from HQ. A transfer to Pretoria followed by Beijing. It was time to bury Addis Ababa and prepare for Pretoria and Beijing. This was a little too much uncertainty all at once.

But this proposal did not last. We would be transferred to Pretoria but would then go on to Zagreb. We were rather pleased with this suggestion. Zagreb is a very comfortable city to live in and Croatia a beautiful country. The following weeks were spent planning a life in Zagreb.

Since my posting in Pretoria was not expected to last long, we did not move from our home in Johannesburg and I commuted daily to Pretoria. One evening in the office, I received a call from Berne. A committee was in the midst of a meeting and I had been proposed for Moscow. I had until 8.00am the following morning to make my decision. Needless to say, I did not sleep much that night. Yes or no to Moscow? The result of a sleepless night was a yes. We were heading to a country that failed to ignite enthusiasm. Hard climate and hard people. As we had been taught by western media.

This move presented a dilemma. What were we to do with our two German Shepherds? We could not take them to a small city apartment in Moscow. But God's mercy prevailed. Not long before we were due to leave, a couple rang at our home: "Did you pick up two German Shepherds from an animal shelter four years ago? Are we in the right place?" We affirmed. They explained: "They were our dogs. We moved to London and brought them to the animal shelter. Now they had returned and would love to have their dogs back, just in case we would be leaving the country sometime." This came quicker than they'd expected. So our two fury family members could return to their original owners. Thank God.

The transfers took their toll on your soul. Before every relocation I suffered a 'howling phase'. I had to leave my home. Every city that we would spend an average of three years in became a home. But we never had time to mourn after saying goodbye to friends, neighbours, colleagues, hairdresser, doctor and dentist. We were also leaving behind a house and garden, the sounds of birds and animals, the noise of a road or an airport. An express farewell was all time allowed. We boarded a plane, almost always bound for the new post. The very same day, I was allocated my new desk and tasks, introduced to new superiors and colleagues and had to function. These moves were even more difficult for family members. They had to find their own way in the new country, in the new school, the shops, etc and acclimatise to their new unfamiliar environment.

In Moscow, we did not understand the language and nor could we understand the road signs. We would not know in which direction to drive at a junction. Clearly, our brief introduction to Russian prior to our arrival was not enough to begin functioning in the country.

At this point, it must be said that the EDA (Swiss foreign office) is a decent and prudential employer. It looks to ensure that employees with children of school age are sent to posts where there are good German, French or English-speaking schools. The EDA also takes employees' health into consideration, and does not send employees to countries where the environment is not suitable for their or a family member's condition.

I take this opportunity to express my sincere thanks to all my superiors and colleagues from throughout my career. At every new post, I was dependent on their support and collaboration. How else would I have managed to buy a fridge in a foreign land in a foreign language?

# Bribery

## Bribery methods

Bribery was a hot topic in several of the countries I was posted to. Even though it went against my principles, I had to employ bribery from time to time, especially in Sudan. There was no other way. And how did I go about this?

This is how things worked in Khartoum. Alcohol was prohibited in Sudan and hence we were able to bribe government officials with whisky and gin. If the embassy required an import license urgently, for instance for an airfreight shipment containing perishable foods that required refrigeration, and I did not receive it through the normal channels, I would head in person to the respective ministry. I would sit down in the office of the official in charge and exchange pleasantries as was customary in the Arab world. The official would then hand me the stamped authorisation document and I would leave behind a bag with spirits. I never handed over the bag, I simply forgot the bag in that particular office.

If you want to conduct business in Africa – as in most countries around the globe – you need to listen carefully. The word "corruption" is never spoken. At most, one speaks of accommodation.

Let us broach this topic with a concrete example. Asra Importers would like to buy machines from Muller Engineering in Switzerland. The transaction's financing has been arranged. The parties are discussing over tea. The African owner of the company talks about his family. One of his sons is interested in studying in Switzerland. But prior to beginning his studies, he needs to attend a private school to learn German and English. The machine manufacturer assures his African client that he could help. It is understood that this assistance will not be limited to providing a few contacts, but will include financial backing. Then, for instance, the invoice for the machines could be inflated by 20%. Jakob Engineering transfers the difference between the invoiced sum and the real price of the machines to the private school. As one can imagine, these special conditions do not appear on any records.

There is also the accelerator fee. For whatever reason, there are moments when a government agency's services are required. My dossier is on the officer's desk. On a visit to the officer's office to enquire how long I might have to wait for a decision, the officer points to the bottom of a pile of dossiers. The more I am willing to pay – cash in a discreet envelope – the higher my dossier climbs in the pile and hence the shorter time I have to wait for a decision. This system would be tolerable were only a single government agency involved. However, most of the time, multiple authorisations from government agencies are required. During my years in Moscow, the construction of a high rise required some 100 permits. The agencies whose permits were required towards the end of the process would most often charge the highest fees. And since not all developers are willing to obtain all permits prior to beginning construction – an excessively lengthy process – one often sees building sites where construction stopped after completion of the basement or the first floor. Contemporary ruins as it were.

## Creative bargaining power

Bribery often brings results – at least in the short term. This was not quite the case when we installed the telephone and telex connection in the embassy in Khartoum in 1989. We had been waiting for one year for the connection despite all our efforts. The project was at a dead end. No telephone and telex connection implied no swift means of communication with Switzerland. Every time I needed to phone Berne, I would head to the Hotel Akropol and wait in line until my turn came to phone. There would be between 10 and 20 people ahead of me, seated on benches, awaiting their turn. The Hotel Akropol (run by Greeks) paid a telephone operator at the telephone exchange for a few hours a day (normally afternoons from 2pm to 5pm) out of their own pocket. This was our only means of urgent communication with Switzerland. And naturally, all our calls were tapped by both the hotel owner and the secret service.

In October 1989, I was on holiday in Switzerland. I asked a relative who worked at a telephone company if it would be possible to cut the telex connection of Sudan's Permanent Mission in Geneva. Absolutely no problem was his answer. On my return to Sudan, I paid a visit to the Foreign Office in Khartoum and informed them that we would cut their connection in

Geneva should the Swiss Embassy not finally have its connections installed. Miracles do happen. Within 24 hours, we had telephone and telex connections.

Creative bargaining power is also used by counterparts. An example that Westerners often recount from their experiences in Russia. A western company wants to open a shop on a prominent shopping boulevard in Russia and has managed to obtain all necessary permits. Should this not suit an influential local competitor, who was not approached with a bribe, then he can sabotage this venture at will. An effective measure can be to have the street in front of the shop torn open the day after the shop's opening. A large hole is dug directly in front of the entrance to the shop to upgrade the underground cabling. There are no planks placed over the hole and the whole area is closed off to the public – for security reasons, of course – which obviously prevents any shopper from gaining access to the shop. The electricity cabling comes first, followed by water piping and then the sewage pipelines (but this procedure is delayed on the back of delivery problems with the special pipes). With the works finally complete, the hole is filled, but the barriers remain in place awaiting surfacing. Before long, the hole is dug up again. The telephone cabling was forgotten. This process continues until the company, that has still to pay its rent, goes bankrupt, before having been able to welcome a single client.

## My ethical stance

How did I reconcile my use of bribery and my corner cutting with my principles? The answer is simple. I never personally benefited, financially or otherwise, from a single bribe. I used bribes to accelerate matters for the Swiss government or business dealings for companies so as not to have grown old and grey by the time the next hurdle was overcome. The actions I took were never in my personal interest, even long term, since I would soon be transferred to a new posting. Another group of beneficiaries were Swiss aid organisations. I would assist them in importing clothing and medication destined for the needy in a given country. Without the help of officials such as myself, the poorest amongst the population would not have had access to the much-needed medication and medical services.

I could not always use bribes. In Russia, for instance, I could never use bribery. Since I did not speak Russian and had to have everything translated, I did not possess the necessary knowledge of local customs that would have allowed me to adopt such measures.

## No more business with corrupt states

I should like to address a topic at this point. There are a mere 20 to 30 countries in the world designated as having only little corruption. In other words, in a majority of countries there is high to extremely high levels of corruption. I was posted to some of those: Indonesia, Sudan, South Africa and Russia.

The person who believes that for instance a FIFA, that comprises some 180 corrupt states with corrupt national football leagues, can remain a completely non-corrupt organisation, is naïve. In my opinion, Sepp Blatter mastered this tightrope; an absolute 'Mr Clean' could not manage FIFA.

I hear you: "You are exaggerating again, Beat. There is almost no corruption in Europe, America and Oceania." Is this true? Let us begin in Europe. According to the statement above, there would be no corruption in: Russia, Belarus, Romania, Bulgaria, Serbia, Montenegro, Italy, Greece, Spain and Portugal. Do I need to continue?

Can we then trade exclusively with non-corrupt countries? From whom would we buy our coffee, cacao, bananas and oranges, pineapples and avocados? Could we buy cars with parts produced in China, India, Eastern Europe or Korea?

We belong to a world that comprises mainly corrupt states. We can not simply not trade with this majority. What do I advise Swiss business managers who wish to export to such countries? "Engage in business within our borders. You do not know the customs of third countries so hands off. In order to access markets abroad, work together with the Swiss subsidiaries of the companies originating in the country you desire to access."

For a Swiss exporter this would imply selling the Swiss coffee machines to the Swiss subsidiary of a Russian importer. The Russian importer is then responsible for the coffee machines' export out of Switzerland, import into Russia and distribution to clients.

Importing into Switzerland is a little different. Swiss quality standards must be met in order to qualify for sale into the local market. In this case, the importer must convey the quality and social criteria that must be met prior to any purchase. These standards should then regularly be checked by a trustworthy company in the production country.

# Development aid with side effects

## Humanitarian aid in Africa

Humanitarian aid is my favourite topic. I have a very different opinion versus most of my Swiss compatriots. We are bombarded on a daily basis through the media and hundreds of charity organisations with the plight of Africa's poor. Pictures of starving children send a strong message. But have you thought about how sizeable the humanitarian market is in Switzerland? We are talking about some five billion Swiss francs and thousands of jobs. In the internet, I came across 173 Swiss organisations that are involved in development and humanitarian aid. Globally, the African continent is the recipient of hundreds of billions of US Dollars (even after accounting for all the salaries and social security benefits that are paid to employees based in the headquarters of the donor countries). Despite this flow of funds, the predicament of so many people only gets worse, not better. I know the reasons for this only too well.

## How donations finance arms

From our privileged existence in Switzerland, we can hardly imagine how our donations can end up in the hands of the military. However, when a country's legal framework can be exploited or circumvented by the ruling powers, it is indeed possible. I will illustrate how this system worked based on my experience in Sudan. While not identical, the conditions in many countries across Africa are similar.

Currencies like the Swiss franc, the US Dollar, the Euro, the Pound and the Yen are so-called hard currencies. They are in circulation throughout the world. On the other hand, Sudan had a local currency that was only legal tender and convertible in Sudan. The law prescribed that only local currency could held in cash. All payments could only be made in local currency; payments in US Dollars or Euro forbidden. Possessing hard currency was strictly forbidden and the death penalty awaited offenders.

But the aid agencies received their donations in hard currencies, which hence had to be exchanged. These hard currency donations (in francs, dollars, Euro, pound, yen) would be transferred to the Central Bank of Sudan. The aid agencies and international organisations then received their funds in local currency at an exchange rate set by the government. So far, so good.

This is when the ruling class took over. The central bank was under their control. The hard currencies that had been deposited were transferred to accounts abroad. Why abroad? Would you invest in Somalia, Nigeria, Sudan or Burkina Faso? You would probably never see the funds again. So the funds were deposited in bank accounts in Europe and the US. All spending would be executed through these accounts. Some 50% of the funds would be spent on arms and ammunition to ensure they would remain in power, the remaining 50% was considered their personal savings to be invested in their personal pensions. This is how a small share of the donations would end up in the local currency with the aid agencies in the designated country, and the hard currency would be funnelled by means of the local central bank to the country's elite.

But the system was also lucrative for the West. So annually, the African continent was the recipient of hundreds of billions of hard currencies. What I know for sure is that exactly that sum – hundreds of billions of currencies – flowed straight back into the West, where it would be managed on behalf of the elites or spent on luxury goods and real estate and armaments to secure their remaining in power.

## Local currency

This flow of funds into the country and its local currency sparked hyperinflation. And what could you do with this money? Almost nothing. There was so little produced in the region that there was nothing to buy. More than four varieties of vegetables would require lengthy searching with no success guaranteed. We lived in a furnished house provided by the Swiss government. Absolutely every furnishing had been imported via diplomatic consignment. There was absolutely nothing even vaguely equivalent available on the local market.

The aid agencies received a pitifully exchange rate and hence little purchasing power. The central bank's exchange rate was set arbitrarily, as it was not required to reflect a market value. The local Sudanese pound (today: Sudanese dinar) was consequently overvalued. Aid agencies and embassies received just short of five Sudanese pounds per US Dollar. A trading partner often received double that with up to 10 Sudanese pounds per US Dollar. On the black market, 40 Sudanese pounds was the going rate. This was all happening despite the threat of the death penalty for carrying hard currency on one's person.

At the end of our time in Sudan, we had to relieve ourselves of our Sudanese pounds. We went to markets to buy trade beads carrying plastic bags full of money. There was nothing else to buy. Trade beads were once the currency in many African countries. You may recognise these beads from films based in colonial times: beautiful glass pearls in all variations would be exchanged for valuable goods, including gold, slaves and ivory. The beads were made of glass, amber, pearls, coloured stones, indeed anything that was beautiful and rare. We thus bought some 20kg of this African currency that has been on display in our home ever since.

## What can be donated?

If donating cash works so sub-optimally, should we be donating natural produce, the likes of wheat, rice or clothing. A noble approach for the Westerner, but one that failed having overlooked Sudan's bureaucracy and laws. Aid agencies had little chance to import their material goods into the country legally without crippling customs tolls.

Of course, every country has the right to establish their own import restrictions. In Switzerland, there is a list of authorised medication. Any substance that does not feature on the list can not be imported. However, the lists in Sudan – and in particular the execution – had a very different character.

When we imported aid in the form of food, the imagination that went into the creation of formalities that were required for the import of such goods was astonishing. The goods would arrive at customs and placed in interim storage. This led to delays and high storage fees. A horrendous import duty then came as the icing on the cake. This was the best-case scenario. A worse-case scenario would see our goods (foodstuff or medication) deemed out-of-date and we were liable for the cost of their destruction. Of course, nothing was ever destroyed. It would be sold on the market or distributed to hospitals or doctors. In the few stores in the city targeting wealthy locals or foreigners, we would always find sacks of sugar and flour, tins of powder milk, all with a stamp: "Donated by the USA" or "Donated by the EU". What were we to do? We needed to buy food, especially for the families of our employees. And hence, we bought the donated produce. The bulk of the food we ate ourselves was flown in.

A concrete example of material donations: Switzerland donated seven tons of milk powder a year to the Sudan. In 1989, the local authorities requested confirmation that there was no radioactive contamination in the milk powder (following the Chernobyl reactor accident in 1986). We received the requested confirmation from Switzerland, but it was not accepted. The local authorities required an internationally recognised certificate. This certificate was obtained and delivered. But even this requested certificate did not meet the Sudanese authorities' requirements. They declared that they would perform the tests themselves on 700kgs of the merchandise. We heard nothing for quite some time. Then came the announcement that the expiry date had been breached. We were liable for the storage costs in addition to the destruction costs of the milk powder. There was nothing we could do. We paid. And shortly thereafter, yoghurts were available in shops again.

This game was played over and over again with medication and any product that did not meet Sudan's so-called norms. Whenever a product did not meet Sudan's standards – and a reason was always found for such a verdict – the entire shipment was retained or confiscated.

A German shipowner lost patience once in Port Sudan. After weeks of waiting in the port with his cargo of millet, he was to be charged harbour dues and import duties. He tipped the entire shipment of thousands of tons of millet that had been donated to Sudan into the sea and left. For us, such situations were very far from amusing. The ruling class' only goal was to financially profit from all our ventures. They were never concerned that this food or medication could help their own population.

## Why the elites want to maintain the poverty of the masses

The bureaucracy was very obviously managed in such a way as to benefit the ruling elite. Providing for their own population was not the elite's priority, indeed, there are advantages to having as poor a population as possible. A famine would bring donations from around the world into Sudan, the elite financially profited from every famine.

I would go as far as suggesting that the Arab elite did everything within their power to ensure the starvation of the non-Muslims of southern Sudan. Some 300,000 people died annually in the civil war in the day. The Arab northerners were fighting the African southerners. This war was accompanied by a plethora of tribal wars. But hardly anyone in the West was aware of what was happening. The Arab soldiers were rewarded with an African slave (man or woman) whom they could take home. A side note: the Arabic word for a black African, "Abd", is the same as that for a black slave. Back then, there was a Swiss organisation that would buy the slaves and organise their transport back to the south. The going rate back then was USD 200 per slave. This did solve the problem, but rather had the unintended consequence of increasing the trade in slaves. A famine could be useful for Muslim missionaries. The principle was quite simple: "you convert to Islam and we will provide food, schooling and a job."

These structural problems are as prevalent as in a war. One party can not be helped in the medium to long-term if the other party sabotages or exploits your efforts. Since our governments in European strive for "religious neutrality", they often turn a blind eye to the religious hostility being suffered around the world. "Open Doors" – an aid organisation assisting Christians around the world who face religious persecution and discrimination – compiles statistics on persecution. Sudan often features high on the World Watch List (managed 5th place from 200 countries in 2017). In ten countries, the persecution of Christians is extreme, in a further 20, the persecution is very high intensity and in another 20, the persecution is high intensity. The trend is on the rise. And despite this situation, a Swiss consul is required to pursue neutral development aid practice even if a Christian population is severely discriminated against. This is difficult for a Christian civil servant. The situations are always considerably trickier than they appear on the surface. Situations can be further complicated by tribal rivalry, enduring tales of unfair or discriminatory treatment, other religious or cultural differences, the existence of natural resources or simply profiteers exploiting their power.

South Sudan gained independence from the north in 2011. Switzerland played an important role in the creation of this new state. Many problems have not been solved and are smouldering on. Following the decades of civil war, there are so many difficulties and little infrastructure that the government is struggling to establish a functioning administration. The Swiss foreign office continues to assist the population with humanitarian aid alongside support in the building up of a democratic and administrative framework. The goal is to give this young nation the greatest chance at a positive future.

# How consuls engaged on a private basis

The concerned employees of Western embassies engaged in activities that would help especially the discriminated-against southern African population.

When the official channels did not produce results, alternative routes were sought. I turned to importing food and medication in the names of diplomats. Almost all goods for the personal use of embassy staff were imported in shipping containers. This allowed the inclusion of boxes of medicine in the 'diplomatic goods', for instance. These medical shipments would then be passed on to the aid agencies. Convincing the authorities of these individuals' need for so much medication required significant financial persuasion.

In addition to their official functions, embassy staff tried to help in their private sphere. We all employed several people around the house and garden and paid them generously. This was a means of providing a secure income to as many people and their families as possible.

In addition to their salaries, we provided our domestic helpers and gardeners with a hut to live in. These, for local standards, large living quarters were taken advantage of by relatives and they would often have guests living with them, up to 25 per habitation. It was often in our private sphere that we embassy employees could have the biggest impact.

## A different way of dealing with ...

A major problem for humanitarian aid in general was our reliance on a Western way of conducting business, where proactive thinking and efficiency are key pillars. The following two examples provide insight into why this approach often fails in Africa:

Swiss aid workers had developed a 'sun cooker' that used sunshine to cook eliminating the need for a wood fire. The food would be placed in a container with a glass lid and a simple aluminium foil-covered reflecting outer lid. The sun's powerful rays very easily heated the container and cooked the food. There were two constraints; the cooking time was a little longer and one had to keep the glass lid closed at all times throughout the cooking process. It was an ingenious invention, which saved the women the arduous task of collecting firewood from distant forests and obviously reduced deforestation. When the cooker was operated by Westerners, it worked impeccably. However, African women felt obligated to stir the food in the pot during the cooking which obviously prevented it from functioning. The sun cooker also required that one had to begin earlier with the cooking process.

The introduction of machinery and technology to increase production in various fields did not bear fruit. Our aid workers were on-site equipped with Land Cruisers, machines and tools. But all machines that ran on petrol were a problem. The local petrol was not pure enough and did not have sufficient octane. This would damage the machines or even destroy them altogether. For this reason, most people drove diesel cars as they were more resilient. Electricity was also problematic. When we did have electricity, it was not constant, and regularly damaged equipment. Current regulators had to be bought and always used.

Car maintenance was also problematic. If someone had a flat tyre, the car would simply be left at the side of the road. A car window would be wound up not until the window was closed, but until the window winder no longer wound anything. Gear changing was done with such intensity that the gear stick would be broken off. Ferdinand, a close friend from GTZ (German aid organisation that maintained some 650 UN vehicles) was confronted daily with such 'unusual' damages and would only sometimes lose his temper.

Axels were broken regularly as vehicles were always overloaded. But remedial action was not forthcoming. Most cars on the road were pick-ups. The embassy also owned one. Every time you'd stop – which was very often, not just at junctions but for the potholes – a dozen people would jump on the back. I would need to get out and ask half of them to get off again. But as soon as I was back in the driver's cab, they would have jumped back on. So out again to ask them to get off again and try to get the car moving before they'd have jumped back on. This required some patience, needless to say.

## What works

When I am asked if there is any kind of aid that actually works, I say the following:

A missionary hospital that cares for poor Christians in Sudan did manage to relieve pain for example. Furthermore, during the long waiting times, the missionaries would convey elements of the Christian faith. Such clinics have been operating for decades and actually fulfil their goal of helping. They have resigned themselves to the realities on the ground – lost their naivety – and do not get easily frustrated. But even such a hospital can not prevent the donations they survive on flowing through the central bank and financing arms and ammunition.

The granting of microcredits also works well. This applies only to financing of self-sufficiency projects in rural areas, not to the creation of larger companies. But self-sufficiency is also the most important. This system works with women and their projects since women tend to be more careful with the earnings their projects generate. Here too, however, a chunk of the funds flows outside the project when being exchanged into local currency.

Foreigners in Africa can also make a difference with how they spend their money. For this reason, foreigners employ so many people around their homes and offices. Every person they employ provides that person's entire family with a regular income they can survive on.

A quick word on Fairtrade and organic produce: I always recommend the purchase of local produce. Local organic meat actually fosters animal welfare. And the supply chain is short enough to guarantee this. There are considerable challenges to guaranteeing a similar standard and outcome for imported organic goods, especially processed goods. Most of the global supply chains are so complex that there is no labelling to date that comprehensively and credibly guarantees a product's "social or environmental production". Even the most ardent efforts of suppliers for "social production" cannot guarantee that there was not some bullying tactics or corruption somewhere along the supply chain. Buying Fairtrade imports does more for one's conscience than it does for the distant workers.

To conclude, countries that no longer receive development aid begin to organise themselves and develop. An economic system that is in harmony with the African way of doing things is established. An excellent example of this is Ghana.

Humanitarian aid makes sense following a catastrophe. Less so, constant humanitarian and development aid.

I must acknowledge that the EDA has continuously developed its development aid and emergency relief strategy. They have learnt their lessons following decades of engagement. They are fighting abuse with determination to ensure the aid reaches those in need of it.

# How rules of the game differ around the world

In this chapter, I'd like to discuss several topics that would not have been appropriate to include earlier in this book since they appear around the globe.

## How business is conducted around the world

How large corporations conduct business in Western Europe is quite different to how business is conducted in Africa or Asia.

In Western Europe, companies employ salespeople who present the company's product to potential buying companies, negotiate terms and conditions, and then present the contracts to the responsible management member for sign-off. The buying companies employ purchasers who acquaint themselves with the product, discuss the product's features, pros and cons with management before a decision is taken as to buy or not to buy.

It is a very different story in Africa. Such negotiations are conducted by the CEO or company owner in person. Accordingly, the CEO of the Swiss company is expected to attend.

Discussions follow but not simply in an office. The client is invited to a relaxed dinner, preferably at the home of the CEO. The production facilities are also visited.

The third and most important step: things take time, a lot of time. One should never expect to get down to business instantaneously. One begins talking about one's children, hobbies, relatives and upbringing. It takes hours if not days before the product in question is addressed. In addition to the product, a good deal of attention is on after sales service, so guarantee and maintenance. A major strength of Swiss companies is their after sales service. On price alone, they would not be competitive. It is also expected that the CEO is in a position to take all necessary decisions. The final decision is taken and contracts signed on the spot with no place for an internal meeting to finalise details.

The time spent in discussions allows the two parties to get to know each other. However, often these well-to-do business people have other questions beyond the transaction in question. They may be interested in education for their children in Switzerland or the opening of a Swiss bank account. Should we be in a position to support them in these other matters, the transaction becomes a mere formality.

More often than not, the African company CEO travels to Switzerland for the negotiations. Where possible, the invitation includes the travel and accommodation costs for the CEO and his wife. In addition to the negotiation program, excursions to the Titlis or Jungfraujoch are expected. Furthermore, it is assumed that the CEO of the Swiss firm personally join this client throughout his stay, including the excursions. Time and patience are required for a successful transaction. One must not forget that there are other suppliers of similar products on the market. And one must not forget that the CEO's wife is busy shopping and needs time.

The sale of western products to Africa is relatively easy. Transactions require advance payment. African firms are accustomed to pay in advance and then receive the goods. In contrast, buying African goods is complicated. Small African suppliers tend to have difficulty providing higher quantities at the required standard. For this reason, trade is conducted with large-scale landowners. Migros and Coop – Switzerland's two dominant supermarket chains that together account for some 70% of the country's food and drinks sales – for example, require regular shipments of tons of a particular tropical fruit, obviously flawless, and not just when they managed a shipment. Swiss consumers do not appreciate empty shelves.

Negotiating business around getting to know one's business partner is not just common in Africa, but is widespread around the world. The extended business trips to Switzerland are also popular in Russia. A relationship of trust is built and wives enjoy the shopping. However, the Russians do not expect to be escorted on their tourist excursions.

# The power of the media

The power of the media around the world is enormous. What is reported on, is a hot topic. What is not reported on, appears not to exist.

A good example of this is the conflict between Israel and Palestine. Most Swiss media are biased towards the Palestinians in their reporting. If Israel strikes a few buildings in the Gaza Strip with missiles, the media portray a barbaric attack by Israel and condemn the destruction of a school that was hit. The fact that the Palestinians had been firing rockets into Israel for weeks and had hidden its weapons and ammunition in the school is barely, if at all, mentioned. No wonder the Swiss are pro-Palestinian. This illustrates the power of the media and those who have influence on the media especially.

One of the most important ministries in most countries is the Ministry of Information, especially in times of conflict, war and unrest. During a coup, gaining control of the radio and television stations is a key priority. These channels are used to inform the general public – or rather to disinform them.

All governments provide journalists with information. You know the scene; a government spokesperson standing at a lectern addressing a room full of reporters who are taking notes in their notebooks while their colleagues take photos. The question is how free a country's journalists are in their portrayal of the information that they receive from the government. In many countries, people who publish material that the government does not deem agreeable land in prison or simply disappear. In such states, news is knowingly generated. Demonstrations can be organised by the state. All civil servants and their families are obligated to attend. Over time, the propaganda shapes the views of their own population and public opinion globally. I am disturbed when I see the footage of such demonstrations on television without a qualifying commentary.

I am also surprised time and again when the western media fails to highlight deliberate deceitful communication. An example: I was once invited to a meeting with Hassan al Tourabi in Sudan. He was a Sudanese politician, religious leader and spiritual head of the Muslim Brotherhood. Our discussion, or rather al Tourabi's monologue, lasted two hours. He stressed his appreciation of Christianity – he had personally learned German in order to be able to read the original version of Luther's translation of the bible. It was a top priority of his to see Muslims and Christians living together in peace. The reality did not reflect the sentiments he expressed. Al Tourabi had founded the Muslim Brotherhood in Sudan and had been involved in the overthrow of the prime minister Sadiq al Mahdi and his replacement with al Bashir. The lives of Christians in the country has since gone downhill. What is the principle behind this communication: in the Arab culture, it is polite to tell your counterpart what they would like to hear. This is more important than conveying your own opinion. This principle stands, even when such a person moves to Switzerland and is integrated in society. One expressed two views, one for the Swiss that one meets and another for fellow countrymen and supporters.

A country's media reports almost exclusively on domestic affairs and the affairs of a country's important trading partners. Their geographic focus is clearly very selective. Here in Switzerland, our priority list is as follows: Germany, Europe, North America, Middle East, China and Japan. African countries are hardly alluded to, civil wars fought over years appear to awaken little interest. Australia, South America and many countries in Asia are more or less ignored. There is a media outcry when 11 people are killed in an attack in Paris, but you might only find a short article buried in the middle of a newspaper when 200 Christians are massacred over a month in Nigeria. Each country has its geographic focus. In itself, not so bad. However, readers and audiences alike believe they are fully informed.

## World peace

I am always surprised how so many believe that the peoples of the world should live together in peace. It would of course be wonderful. But in every family, at every workplace, in every apartment block, in every association and every political party, there is some measure of strife, conflict or all-out war, be it from time to time or permanent. If it does not work on a small scale, how on earth should it work for the whole world?

# Sub-Saharan Africa: sharing

In rural Sub-Saharan Africa, living in a community is completely different to the way we know it in Europe. The value of the family, the extended family, indeed the entire village community is so much greater than it is in the west.

We also live in families whilst our children are still children or youths. But even early on, there is plenty of individualism, individual development, individual ownership. Old parents are sent to nursing homes and if they are lucky, are paid a visit from time to time. In the past, before the age of social security, families stuck together. In Africa, children are still the pension scheme for their parents. The younger family members take care of the elderly family members. This is especially true in rural areas. In the meantime, the majority live in apartment blocks in the cities – in apartments sufficient space for a small family only. But the care of family members is deep-rooted in the culture.

Everything is shared, and not just in the family, but amongst relatives and the village community. A relative in need moves in with a family member as opposed to simply being fed a meal or given some emergency money and sent on their way. One of our domestic helpers in Sudan used to have up to 25 people staying in his hut. Most would sleep outside on mats with a stone for a pillow. He provided these people refuge from the civil war in the south. Due to this social cohesion, there are many fewer mentally ill people in Africa compared to in the West. In our region, almost every person is psychologically impaired in some way. Another reason for the lack of psychological problems is that the battle to stay alive leaves little space for psychological complaints. A journey of self-discovery is simply irrelevant when you do not know how you'll feed yourself tomorrow.

The African philosophy of "who has, shares" goes much further than we in the West can imagine. I attended an investment symposium in Johannesburg. Western countries were being encouraged to invest in various industrial sectors as part of their development aid. I asked a provocative question to the audience: "why should Western business people invest when the local African business people do not?" It went quiet. There was no explanation. Conservative estimates of declared foreign assets that Africans hold stood at 600 billion US Dollars. And that back in 2002. The effective foreign assets by the continent's ruling class is considerably higher. At this event, I discussed with a representative of the World Bank from West Africa. I inquired as to how he was welcomed on visits to his home. Was everyone in his village proud of his stellar career? His answer came rather unexpected: "I can no longer go home. The villagers expect me to arrive with multiple truckloads of millet or wheat, spare car parts and pumps." He had been living in Washington DC for years, had adopted Western customs and was no longer willing to share with his fellow villagers. Understandable on the one hand, disappointing on the other.

Aware of these circumstances, one starts to understand why African rulers tend to favour their own tribe. It is certainly generally accepted practice; the favouritism demanded by your own tribe and mistrustfully observed by all other tribes. The latter are lying in wait for the first opportunity to turn the tables and reap the benefits of a member of their own tribe ascending to the throne.

Extrapolating on this principle, we can better understand what refugees anticipate on their arrival in the West. The villagers collect money to be able to finance the trip to Europe of one villager. Once up and running in Europe, he is expected to send money home on a regular basis. And there can be considerable pressure exercised. I know the personal situation of an Eritrean woman who lives in Switzerland. She apparently sent too little money back to Eritrea so her sister was murdered. She returned home for her sister's funeral, despite this practice being prohibited as refugees are seeking refuge from the persecution in their country of origin. My friend returned to Switzerland with severest burns. She had boiling water poured over her on her departure. On her arrival in Switzerland, she was transferred by ambulance to Zurich's university hospital to undergo emergency treatment. The Eritreans have their methods of collecting money abroad.

I lived seven years on the African continent and came to appreciate so many aspects, not least the people. I understand why so many wish to go to Western Europe. We have enough in Western Europe, too much in their eyes. Sharing is deeply entrenched in their culture. So they come to Western Europe in droves to collect their share of the surplus. This makes complete sense in their eyes.

# The ball that unites the world

I was very lucky to be a part of the build-up to a Football World Cup (South Africa 2010) and a Winter Olympics (Sochi 2014) during my last two postings.

Moscow was from the very start my most labour-intensive posting. Following the announcement that Sochi would be hosting the Winter Olympics, the months prior to the announcement felt like a Sunday stroll in the park. Billions in investments would be required up front to host these events. Sochi was not much more than a village. The entire infrastructure requirements for the Olympics had to be built from scratch. I travelled to Sochi to meet with the people in charge, accompanied by a member of my team at the embassy. We informed them about the essential know-how that many Swiss companies have in the fields of winter sports, hotel industry, water treatment, etc. I invited the most important decision-makers to Zurich where I organised a congress at which 200 Swiss companies could present their products and services. It would appear to have been a successful event considering the share that Swiss companies received of the 50 billion US Dollar budget.

Incidentally, the venue for a sporting event is chosen based on the fulfilment of logistical requirements set by FIFA or the Olympic Committee: stadiums with capacity for 40,000 to 100,000 spectators and sufficient accommodation for all participants and spectators (as of 30,000 beds within an acceptable distance from the venue). In addition, transportation (road, rail and busses) to and from the stadiums, arrival and departure capacity at the airport(s) (expansion of airport infrastructure) and catering for the spectators with up to 200,000 meals per day must be guaranteed. Needless to say, 2% sport and 98% business.

Many believe that Putin 'bought' the Olympics. I shall not comment on this topic. But it would not be the first time that money flowed to secure the hosting of the games. Some of you may remember the Sion 2006 bid for the Winter Olympics. Sion had the most comprehensive dossier and it was clear to all commentators that Sion would win the contest to host. And who won? Turin...!

Something else I have learned during my time working around the world is the truly global popularity of football. The sport had been starved in Africa for many years. But this has changed dramatically in the last few decades.

I watched a film in the FIFA museum in Zurich. It documented the influence FIFA had had on the African continent. Africans did not keep their common spaces in order. Everything would be thrown away. Their 'gardens' resembled rubbish dumps and no one cared. When FIFA introduced football training, new standards were established. Qualified football trainers were provided along with football jerseys and shorts, and real leather footballs. But before training could begin, gardens, roads and pavements had to be cleared of rubbish. Truly Swiss (Blatter)-style influence. Would it not be a fair question to ask whether FIFA has not done more for Africa than all the government and NGO aid agencies?

# Looking forward to retirement?

## Grumpy old man or active, engaged senior citizen

After 30 exciting years abroad, I was looking forward to my retirement. We returned from our last posting in Moscow and were settling down in a new home back in Switzerland.

And then came that scene worthy of a film. Beat Moser had played the roles of Consul General, Embassy Councillor and Managing Director of the Swiss Business Hub in Moscow. From one day to the next, he had a new role: pensioner, househusband, gardener, chauffeur and bored walker at the Greifensee. Did anyone take notice of him? Hardly. He was a pensioner and looked like all the other pensioners. And he had difficulty coming to terms with this new role.

Looking forward to retirement? Really? Are you forgetting that your partner might not want you all the time in the house all of a sudden and not wish to accompany you on excursions every day? She does not wish to change her daily routine. This is typical amongst recent retirees. Is there a solution?

In my case, it was illness. I could not come to terms with my new role as a pensioner. I lost my balance – also physically. I had a so-called sudden acute loss of hearing. The equilibrium organ in my right ear had packed up.

My wife and I found another escape from the retirement dilemma: two months after my retirement, she got a job. My new role was twofold; househusband and patient.

I was faced with an additional and more unique problem having just returned from abroad. I had no local network. No club where I'd been a member for many years that could help me deal with my new role. No friends who would ask me over for a visit. Even my children were living in different countries abroad at the time. I began organising events for the Swiss Chamber of Commerce but had to give up the role to avoid having my early retirement benefits cut.

In 2009, I founded a gospel choir that I also conducted. This did me a lot of good. I had found a role where I was with people who considered me a 'whole' person. And with this revived self-confidence, I began taking on all kinds of jobs.

I founded a company where I offered consulting on international networking. I conducted location promotion activities at the company "Moser Location Promotion" (Molopro GmbH). Amongst other activities, I helped Russian companies establish Swiss subsidiaries.

In no time, my days were full. There were so many jobs that needed doing where I could support or where my assistance would be requested as a ("you now have the time") pensioner.

## My love of music

The passage contains an explanatory parenthesis about music in my life. I have a passion for music. It all began with my violin lessons when I was in primary four. My teacher played the violin. I was spellbound. How could I find a way of spending more time with her or even having her all to myself? It was simple. I began taking violin lessons with her. One hour every week. She had no idea of my secret reason for having taken up the violin but she managed to awaken my love of music.

Following compulsory schooling, I went to teacher training college. Here I had my first experiences conducting. In 1968, I conducted the premiere of Helmut Schilling's "Earth, Fire, Water, Air" symphony at a graduation ceremony. At college and later in Solothurn's city orchestra, I played the violin and the viola.

How I became the conductor of the Jodlerklub Luterbach (club of yodelers) is special. I was only 22 years old and a teacher. I was invited three times by the president of the yodeler club in person to conduct his choir. I turned the invitation down twice on the grounds that I did not know the genre, which was true. What I did not say was that I was not really a fan of the genre either. Upon the third invitation, I agreed to listen in on a choir practice. Not so. I had barely arrived when the president handed me the notes and instructed me to conduct. Just like that. That is how I became conductor of the Jodlerklub Luterbach. I came to appreciate the singers over time and with that also the music. When they sang of a sunset, of mountains, of cows or of pastures, it came from the heart. Funnily enough, there are no songs about pigs, goats or chickens. They were always affectionate amongst each other – as affectionate as men were amongst each other back in the day. To say nothing bad was a compliment. We won first prize at the North Western Swiss yodeler festival held in Basel-Landschaft. They obviously sung in traditional dress, me included.

I was also active in various choirs abroad. The Africans have tremendous voices. And there was a harmony amongst their voices that I never experienced anywhere else. A singer would begin a new song and within seconds the choir was singing it with four voices. And no one singing out of tune.

I sang in the "Soweto Gospel Choir" in South Africa. On my first visit, I asked where the tenors sung. Tenors are everywhere. The choir was organised into quartets with a soprano, an alto, a tenor and a bass in each. And they were spread out everywhere. This rendered the choir considerably more harmonious. And something else: every choir member had to know their own voice. It was not easy to sing in an African choir. I struggled with pronunciation, movement and measure.

When I took lessons at the "Fuba School of Music" located in downtown Johannesburg, where whites never dared to venture, I got to know the diversity of their music. Every ethnic group has their own sound, rhythm and dance. I did my best, but needless to say, I was a bit of a laughing stock to the young students (in the nicest of ways). I simply could not move as they did. Very few non-Africans can. On the other hand, they were very quick to learn Swiss songs. Amongst others, I taught them a very traditional song "Wenn eine tannigi Hose het und hageuechig Strümpf", a typical Swiss canon, and it sounded great.

On my return to Switzerland, I founded a choir singing African songs. There is quite a difference in vocal strength between the average Swiss voice and that of an African. There are also differences in how we move and our facial expression. It took quite some persuasion to create a cheerful and vibrant gospel choir.

## The big blow

After four years as an active pensioner came the big blow. Looking forward to retirement? I could live with the acute loss of hearing and balance. Now I was diagnosed with cancer. In May 2013, I received the verdict: cancer of the oesophagus. This was tough. Even now, I need to spread my calorie intake over six meals a day and do not tolerate many foodstuffs. What a way to begin retirement.

Prior to the diagnosis, I was very active. The company, the choir, and an abundance of odd jobs. But was this God's plan? Running from one meeting to the next, trying to be in all places at the same time? Had God another plan for me? Today, a few years later, I know the answer. He was always at my side. God was generous with me. He sought me, but I thought I didn't need Him. I was successful. I was too busy to listen to Him. So He gifted me this sickness to bring me back to Him, my Creator.

My oesophageal cancer was so severe that I had no choice but to immediately quit all activities, including liquidating my company. These were hard times, indeed very hard times, but also infinitely liberating. God had a new purpose for me; to be grateful. Grateful for everything that I have.

Of course, it is not always easy to deal with my ailments on a day-to-day basis. Some days are better, other less good. It is my mind that often has difficulty enduring dealing with symptoms. There are days when I bemoan my fate with God. But then come times when gratitude returns for all that God has given me.

The following is an account of my emotional state in my first year, from cancer diagnosis, through treatment and rehab, to a return to a new normality back at home.

## From shock to gratitude

The first 365 days in the life of a cancer sufferer, written in summer 2014.

Wednesday before Pentecost, 2013: I awake to a man in a white overall. He is a gastroenterologist. I was sent to him by my GP as I was having difficulty swallowing. He told me that I had cancer. He drew a picture of the tumour in my oesophagus. Do you have any questions? I was crying and shook my head. Then you are free to get dressed and leave.

With tear-filled eyes I left the practice by the back door. Back home, I wrote an email to my wife, my children and my brothers. I was unable to speak.

Around midday, I took a train and then a bus to Ländli (Oberägeri, central Switzerland) where I'd booked a stay over the Pentecost weekend. Tears accompanied me throughout the journey, at reception, in my room. I pulled myself together for the course in which I'd enrolled myself and made no mention of the finding. Only on my departure did I speak with a deaconess about my predicament and said I felt like a cry baby. She assured me that this was a completely normal reaction to such news. Jesus had cried. It did me good.

Back home, the tears did not subside. At the end of June, a port was operated into my chest at Zurich's University Hospital – I suffered from hospital phobia and discharged myself. July saw the beginning of chemotherapy, August radiotherapy. I took to the treatment very badly. I was constantly sick, very often in tears. I did not understand why I was so sad. Death was a notion I was comfortable with, I believed in relief and an afterlife in heaven. Was I mourning the loss of my father, my mother, my sister? Was it the all-too frequent farewells around the world as we moved home every three years?

During these tearful months, I asked friends and acquaintances not to visit, not to call. They all respected this wish. I thank them all heartily. I was in no position to speak. I could only cry.

In July, God bestowed me with a wise, old pastoral caregiver. I spoke of my helplessness, my hospital phobia, my constant deep sorrow, ... He had but one answer; unrelenting, daily prayer:

Thank you, Father, for holding me.

I went to him in August. I'd suffered the chemotherapy and the radiotherapy. And his answer: unrelenting, daily prayer. Thank you, Father, that I am in your arms. In September and October, I went to him and received the same answer. Every day, I prayed in front of a picture of two hands holding an hourglass that he had given me. You are in God's arms during your limited life on earth.

November came and another visit with the surgeon. The date of my operation was postponed from December 2013 to January 2014 – thanks to God's intervention. I was able to recover before the major operation – including a week in Ländli during the run-up to Christmas.

I celebrated the festive season in the presence of closest family. I was surrounded by their love, and their desire that I regain my health.

January 7, I was admitted to the University Hospital of Zurich. On January 8, I underwent the eight-hour surgery. My wife was by my side as I awoke in intensive care. My son had spent the whole day in the chapel of the hospital. My other children and many people in Switzerland and around the world were praying for my wellbeing.

The operation was a success. My oesophagus had been removed and replaced by my stomach, pulled up and sewn into place – a complicated and delicate operation. I awoke amid a myriad of tubes and monitoring equipment. And I prayed: thank you, Father, that I am in your arms. I was thirsty but was not permitted to drink. I was otherwise fine.

Two weeks later, I was transferred to rehabilitation. Here I was to be schooled for three weeks on how to eat – little and at regular intervals – and how to walk again. I contracted a stomach virus and on my discharge from rehabilitation, I was readmitted to the University Hospital of Zurich for a further eight days.

Back home, the several month-long rehabilitation phase was not easy for my family, nor for myself. I did not enjoy being a patient. But I was lovingly cared for. Today, six months after the operation, I feel surprisingly well. I am able to eat almost everything, albeit in very small quantities. I am keeping my weight up – some 10kgs below my pre-illness levels. There are no signs of cancer cells in my body in my recent tests. I have begun to plan for the future again.

One year since the cancer was discovered, my life has completely changed. My relationship with God has gotten immeasurably closer. My daily Bible reading and prayer have brought me intimacy with Him. During the months of acute discomfort and sadness, I acknowledged my many sins and asked for forgiveness. Today, I am another person, happy and content (the meaning of my first name). When now tears come, they are tears of thanks and of happiness. God blessed me with an illness so that I could get my life and my relationship with Him in order. I am so deeply thankful for the hardship I had to endure and especially for the help our Creator provided. I have not stopped praying to this day: thank you, Father, that I am in your arms.

## Victim of circumstances

I would like to address a topic that bothers me, that I see in myself and those around: namely how good we are at complaining and how little time we have for gratitude. This is something very prominent in our Western society.

Most people have a tendency to complain more than to praise or be grateful for. I very often hear: "My husband died. It is awful that he had to suffer this illness. I am so lonely now." It is very seldom that I hear: "My husband died. I am so grateful for the 40 wonderful years that we spent together." How often do people get in contact with a pastoral caregiver or friends to complain about all that is not good. In some cases, there may be some discussion on how to deal with similar problems in the future. Far less often is a mentor engaged to examine one's own shortcomings and to approach God to ask for forgiveness. It would appear that most people consider themselves rather as victims than perpetrators. Other people, an illness, circumstances or fate are responsible for one's state of affairs, but never oneself.

In need of more examples? Even prison inmates are only the victims of miscarriages of justice. This is something I regularly heard in Strasbourg. A drug dealer is on the train crossing the border into France. The customs officers recognise the drug addicts and some hashish is found on their person. The officers would then find a larger quantity of hashish above a ceiling panel in the toilets or otherwise well-hidden somewhere in the train. The drug addict would then also be charged with the smuggling of the larger quantity and end up in prison. They obviously denied everything and complained of a miscarriage of justice.

Even Christians often feel like victims. I met such a victim in a holiday resort. He introduced himself as a pastor. Interesting, I thought. And then I spent the next four hours listening to his woes. He saw himself exclusively as a victim. Unbelievable. He had worn the number two all his life. His first-rate education, his good health at over fifty years of age and all other aspects of a live of privilege were simply overlooked. His wife dominates the relationship (the case in 80% of marriages, so not uncommon), his mother, who was set to bequest a few hundred thousand Swiss francs, does not want to die, and his wife does not want to share her inheritance with him (absolutely her right since this is her personal property). This poor pastor. He is just a victim.

I was also living as a victim for decades. Only midst in my sickness did I realise to what extent I'd excused myself throughout my life, and to what extent I'd blamed others or the circumstances. During my oesophageal cancer treatment, I spent many, many hours alone in bed. My thoughts wandered and went around in circles. There were more and more situations where I saw my own complicity. Many were minor issues that I'd simply swept under the carpet. But they did exist: how I had been dismissive towards people or ideas, how I had provoked, how I had been stubborn or how I had played a situation to my advantage. How often had I neglected to do the right thing? For decades, I had had so much on my plate and been in a position of authority, I had simply not found the time to analyse my actions. It was easy to avoid such penetrating thoughts. And despite this, my subconsciousness was eating at me. The deeper my relationship to God became during my sickness, the more such instances resurfaced. And not just in my professional life, but everywhere. It suddenly became very apparent to me: I had not simply been a victim, but had at least been a perpetrator half my life. This realisation was essential. Only now could I ask God for forgiveness for my transgressions. Only once I'd come to terms with my deeds and thoughts and admitted my guilt, did I experience inner, and to some extent, exterior healing. This was my salvation.

Why am I writing this? For some, as an example of how enriching and liberating a personal relationship with the Almighty God is. For others, to encourage them to see the good things in life and to be grateful.

Because, if you spend your life seeing yourself only as a victim, you will never be content.

This topic remains relevant. In recent weeks, I have been faced again with the question as to whether I am a victim or a perpetrator. In recent years, I have been taking too high doses of certain medicines. These had led to an onset of dementia. How easy would it be to blame circumstances or the prescribing doctors. Then I would only be a victim. But in reality, I am a perpetrator, at the very least accomplice. It was I who took the tablets, and I who requested more packages of tablets. It was a simple solution that I regret today. Coming off the tablets was extremely challenging. But I was trying, with God's help, to free myself of them. And I am ever grateful for the support and prayers of a wide circle of fellow Christians.

## How thankful we should be

However I am feeling on a given day, there is so much I can be thankful for. Here in Switzerland, we do not only have an abundance of food, beautiful clothes and luxury goods. We have so much that we take for granted, that we should not. During my time abroad, I have seen what it is like not to have these things.

It was very eloquently put in a sermon held for the Federal Day of Thanksgiving, Repentance and Prayer. The sermon has been provided by Stefanie Thoms, a theologian and publisher:

"We have a functioning waste disposal system, we do not have mounds of stinking rubbish in front of our doors. We have a good sewage system, we need not use a smelly outhouse. We have heating. We can even take warm showers. All we need to do is turn a tap and not walk 10 minutes or even two hours to the nearest well. We can drink tap water, and it does not taste of chlorine. We have electricity. Our houses do not collapse. In modern houses, one can hardly even hear the neighbours.

When we fall ill, we can visit the doctor. If we get toothache, there are dentists to care for us. We have enough medication that we are able to buy. Doctors here can treat many ailments that could otherwise leave you handicapped for the rest of your life in other countries. And in the case of a disability, the state provides funds to cover cost of living and cost of care. We have insurances that, in most cases, cover the costs of treatments so that we do not end up on the street should we fall seriously ill. Old age does not mean being kicked out onto the street to starve. We have retirement homes that the state pays if necessary.

We have a good legal system. If you are in the right, a court will rule in your favour and if you have committed an offence, you will be reprimanded. We do not live under the rule of despotism. The state protects its citizens. We have freedom of opinion. We have the right to vote. We have the right to get involved in politics. All is done to eliminate corruption from processes across society.

Schooling is free of charge. Parents are not required to spend half their salaries on school fees and not have enough to eat as a consequence. The nation strives to provide all citizens with equal opportunities. We live in a technocratic society where status is not inherited. Hard work pays off.

We have laws that protect us in the workplace. We can not be forced to work more than 12 hours a day. Breaks are mandatory. There are workers' unions. At the end of the day, we have some change in the purse, we can even put something on the side or go on a holiday.

We have an excellent transportation network. And we have a state with sufficient capacity that they can afford to see that we observe traffic rules. These traffic rules are adopted to reduce the number and seriousness of accidents. Our nation even has enough money to take care of nature. We have renaturation and green power. There is animal welfare. Our country is located neither in the artic or the desert, our land is arable, green and beautiful. We do not have contaminated regions.

We have been spared war for decades. No war that has destroyed all that we have painstakingly built up, that has spread pain and anguish, that has physically and psychologically ruined the lives of our citizens.

We are free to practice our Faith. We are permitted to congregate, to write and read books about Christianity and talk about it. We are free to read the Bible. We do not face prejudice in the workplace or in politics based on our Christian beliefs.

We have a God who sent His Son to the earth so that we would be freed. Jesus died and rose for us so that our path to God is free.

This was a long list. Of course, not everything is this rosy. A well-meant law can backfire. There will be people that fall through the welfare safety net. Much in our social system is leading to increased loneliness. People are increasingly subjected to "you can manage alone, there is no God." I am acutely aware of this and that is why I can shrug it off. I want to see the good and be grateful.

Even negative things can be seen from various angles. 'Gratefulness for the advanced' can look like this (taken from a note on the door of a retirement home): "I am grateful for the mess that I need to clean up after a party, because it means I was surrounded by friends. I am grateful for the taxes I have to pay, because that means I am not unemployed. I am grateful for the lawn I have to mow, for the windows I need to clean and the gutter that I need to repair, because that means I have a home. I am grateful for the complaints I hear about our government, because that means that we have a freedom of opinion and expression. I am grateful for the piles of washing, because that means that I have loved ones with me. I am grateful for the alarm clock that rings early in the morning, because that means I am alive and have responsibilities."

## Looking back

I had an interesting and blessed life. In hindsight, I realise that the Almighty was protecting me throughout. And this whether or not I was in a close relationship with Him.

Time and again, God would let me know that He was there. The first time in my youth. I came to the Lord in 1965, in Moscia in the Ticino whilst at teacher training college. But over time, my interest in Him petered out. Upon the death of my father in 1980, and on my mother's deathbed in 1985, a helplessness led me back to Him. In most countries I was posted in, our family were regulars at the local church. I was active in church life and enjoyed the teachings of many wonderful and impressive pastors. But time and again, I wanted to master my own life.

When I was diagnosed with oesophageal cancer in 2013, my interrupted connection to the Almighty was re-established. As powerless as I felt during chemotherapy, radiotherapy and following the surgery to remove my oesophagus, I had never before felt in my life. I could not do anything myself. Without a pastoral caregiver, I doubt I would have survived this time. My trips to the Christian convalescence facility Ländli in Oberägeri (Central Switzerland) did me a lot of good. I realised that this special place was blessed. I experienced my closest encounters with God there.

Finally, I should like to thank my wife, my children with families, my brothers with families, my relatives and my friends from within and outside the church for all that they have done for me. I should also like to thank all those who have prayed for me during my times of crisis. I thank the deaconesses at Ländli and in Berne and my pastoral caregiver, Reinhard Egg. You all helped me to accept my new, blessed life that the Creator bestowed on me. I am grateful every single day. May the Lord bless and protect you.

## Appendix: Resume

| | |
|---|---|
| 1949 | Year of birth. Grew up in Richigen, Canton of Berne, Switzerland |
| 1965 – 1969 | Teacher Training College Hofwil and Berne, Primary School Teaching Diploma |
| 1969 – 1970 | Substitute teaching positions at primary schools, 6 months on Kibbutz |
| 1970 – 1971 | Primary school teacher, Solothurn |
| 1971 – 1974 | Primary school teacher, Feldbrunnen |
| 1974 | Entered Swiss Foreign Service (EDA) |
| 1975 – 1976 | Consulate General in Manchester (consular stagiaire) |
| 1976 – 1980* | Consulate General in Sydney (consular secretary) |
| | *August – December 1979 in Jakarta (head of consular section) |
| 1980 – 1983 | Consulate General in Marseille (consular assistant) |
| 1983 – 1986 | Embassy in London (consular assistant) |
| 1986 – 1988 | Consulate in Strasbourg (vice consul) |
| 1988 – 1991 | Embassy in Khartoum (vice consul) |
| 1991 – 1994 | Consulate General in Melbourne (consul) |
| 1994 – 1997 | Embassy in Oslo (consul) |
| 1997 – 2001 | Swiss Foreign Office in Berne (diplomatic staff member) |
| 2001 – 2003 | Consulate General in Johannesburg (assistant consul general) |
| 2003 – 2005 | Embassy in Pretoria (embassy counsellor, head of trade section) |
| 2005 – 2008 | Embassy in Moscow (embassy counsellor, head of Swiss Business Hub) |
| June 2008 | early retirement |
| 2009 – 2013 | founder of Molopro GmbH, a location promotion company |

Stefan Schweizer

# Staatstheorien der Aufklärung

Theorien der Demokratie und der Gesellschaftsanalyse

Stefan Schweizer

# Staatstheorien der Aufklärung

www.europäischer-hochschulverlag.de

Schweizer, Stefan
**Staatstheorien der Aufklärung**
*Theorien der Demokratie und Gesellschaftsanalyse*

1. Auflage 2009
ISBN: 978-3-941482-27-2
© Europäischer Hochschulverlag GmbH & Co. KG,
Bremen, 2009.
www.europäischer-hochschulverlag.de
Alle Rechte vorbehalten
Umschlagbild: Daniel Nikolaus Chodowiecki „Aufklärung", 1791 (Ausschnitt)

Die Deutsche Bibliothek verzeichnet diesen Titel in der Deutschen Nationalbibliografie. Bibliografische Daten sind unter http://dnb.ddb.de abrufbar.

*Für Constantin*

Inhaltsverzeichnis

1. **Bedeutung der Staatstheorien** — 3
2. **Gemeinsamkeiten der Vertragstheorien** — 11
3. **Die Epoche der Aufklärung als Wiege der Demokratie** — 15
   3.1 Soziopolitische Merkmale der Aufklärung — 16
   3.2 Aufklärung und Bildung — 19
4. **Hobbes' Staatstheorie** — 21
   4.1 Biographischer und historischer Kontext — 21
   4.2 Menschenbild, Naturzustand und Vertragsabschluss — 22
   4.3 Nach Vertragsschluss: Der Staat — 24
   4.4 Der Souverän und die Untertanen: Vom Zweck des Staats — 25
   4.5 Organisierung staatlicher Gewalt — 26
5. **Lockes Staatstheorie** — 29
   5.1 Biographischer und historischer Kontext — 29
   5.2 Menschenbild und Naturzustand — 31
   5.3 Vertragsabschluss — 32
   5.4 Ziel der Staatsbildung — 33
   5.5 Organisierung der staatlichen Gewalt und Staatsform — 34
   5.6 Fazit — 35
6. **Montesquieus Staatstheorie** — 36
   6.1 Biographischer und historischer Kontext — 36
   6.2 Menschenbild — 37
   6.3 Geschichtsbild und Sozialstruktur — 37
   6.4 Organisierung staatlicher Gewalt — 38
   6.5 Staatsform — 40
   6.6 Kulturrelativismus — 41

7. Rousseaus Staatstheorie — 43
  7.1 Biographischer und historischer Kontext — 43
  7.2 Menschenbild und Naturzustand — 44
  7.3 Vertragsschluss und Ziel der Staatsbildung — 45
  7.4 Organisierung des Staats — 46
  7.5 Inhaber der staatlichen Gewalt — 47
  7.6 Staatsform — 49

8. Hobbes und der „Große Lauschangriff" — 50

9. Anwendungsbeispiel Hobbes und Locke: Fallbeispiel Speichelprobe — 63

Literatur — 71

# 1. Bedeutung der Staatstheorien

Das Thema Staatstheorien bezieht sich auf eines der wichtigsten Gebiete der staatsbürgerlichen Erziehung und damit der stabilen freiheitlich-demokratischen Grundordnung überhaupt. Staatstheorien sind in verschiedenen Ausprägungen vorhanden und insofern sind Selektionskriterien und Begründungen erforderlich. Die Staatstheorien der Aufklärung werden zu Recht als maßgeblicher Einflussfaktor der heutigen westlichen Demokratieformen gesehen. Innerhalb der Aufklärung gibt es eine Kanonbildung der Vertrags- und Staatstheorien: Hobbes, Locke, Montesquieu und Rousseau besitzen seit geraumer Zeit einen festen Platz darin.

Hobbes war der erste Vertragstheoretiker. Er argumentierte mit einem pessimistischen, aber zur Rationalität fähigen Menschenbild, welches die Begründung und Legitimierung staatlicher Gewalt deutlich vor Augen führt. Lockes optimistisches Menschenbild verbindet sich hingegen mit den Grundgedanken liberalen Wirtschaftens. Außerdem ist bei Locke bereits die Gewaltenteilung in nuce erkennbar. Die Gewaltenteilung ist das herausragende Merkmal des französischen Staatstheoretikers Montesquieu, welcher insofern bis heute als zentrales Vorbild westlicher Demokratien gelten darf. Weniger unumstritten ist Rousseau, der radikal eine Identität von Herrschern und Beherrschten dachte. Die politischen Erfahrungen der Vergangenheit haben gezeigt, dass gegenüber solchen idealistischen Demokratievorstellungen Vorsicht geboten ist. Zur ausführlichen Begründung der Relevanz der genannten vier Staats- und Vertragstheoretiker wird an dieser Stelle auf die unten stehenden Einzelkapitel verwiesen.

Zwischen Demokratie und politischer Bildung herrscht ein enger und systematischer Zusammenhang.[1] Demokratie bedeutet dabei gleichzeitig Lebens-, Gesellschafts- und Herrschaftsform.[2] Nicht zuletzt aus dieser fundamentalen und umfassenden Bedeutung für das Zusammenleben in unserer Gesellschaft rechtfertigt sich die Relevanz des Themas Staatstheorien als Gegenstand einer wissenschaftlichen Abhandlung. Den Leserinnen und Lesern soll die exorbitante Relevanz des Themas für unser heutiges gesellschaftspolitisches Zusammenleben vor Augen geführt werden. Historisches Denken ist immer fragmentarisch und perspektivisch. Es verlangt Genauigkeit im Denken und das Aushalten von Mehrdeutigkeit.[3] Dieses Desiderat wird durch Staatstheorien der Aufklärung zur Gänze eingelöst.

Beim Thema Staatstheorien wird sowohl Historizitätsbewusstsein als auch das politische Bewusstsein gefördert. Historizitätsbewusstsein meint „die Einsicht, dass Verhältnisse nicht gleich bleiben, sondern sich in der Zeit verändern […] Historischer Wandel lässt sich erst erfahren, wenn man längere Zeiträume in den Blick nimmt und Vergleiche vor-

---

[1] Massing, P., Demokratie-Lernen oder Politik-Lernen, S. 161
[2] Schiele, S., Politische Bildung neu vermessen?, S. 13
[3] Günther-Arndt, H., Historisches Lernen und Wissenserwerb, S. 26

nimmt."[4] Dieser wissenschaftliche Aufsatz beschäftigt sich mit dem geschichtlichen Bewusstsein, da die Staatstheorien zur Zeit der Aufklärung die Einsicht in die Änderung der Verhältnisse ermöglichen und somit die Basis für Vergleichbarkeit, z.B. mit heute, herstellen. Der Vergleich moderner politischer Systeme lässt sich durch einen Rekurs auf Staatstheorien der Aufklärung optimieren. So kann man in der Schweiz direktdemokratische Elemente à la Rousseau und in Deutschland repräsentative Strukturen wie bei Locke identifizieren. Politisches Bewusstsein bedeutet gegenüber dem Historizitätsbewusstsein „die allgemeine Einsicht, dass menschliche Gesellschaften durch Herrschaftsverhältnisse bestimmt sind, und die Fähigkeit, solche Strukturen zu erkennen und analysieren."[5] An dieser Bestimmung menschlicher Gesellschaften durch Herrschaftsverhältnisse und deren Begründung setzt dieser Aufsatz an. Die Aneignung nachhaltiger Kenntnisse ist beispielsweise durch „Verarbeiten, Ordnen und Vergleichen unter bestimmten Fragestellungen (z.B. Menschenbild und Herrschaftsverständnis bei Hobbes, Locke und Rousseau)"[6] möglich.

Geschichte meint zudem die Vergegenwärtigung des Vergangenen.[7] Insofern impliziert die Beschäftigung mit Staatstheorien der Aufklärung deren Vergegenwärtigung. Wie verhält es sich aber mit

---

[4] Sauer, M., Geschichte unterrichten, S. 16
[5] Sauer, M., Geschichte unterrichten, S. 16
[6] Grammes, T., Exemplarisches lernen, S. 58 f.
[7] Gies, H., Geschichtsunterricht, S. 107

der Politischen Ideengeschichte? Zwischen den Begriffen der politischen Theorie, Ideengeschichte und Staatstheorie besteht ein enger Zusammenhang. So kann man festhalten,[8] dass Politische Theorie den Oberbegriff einer politikwissenschaftlichen Teildisziplin darstellt. Ein Zweig der Politischen Theorie ist die Klassische Politische Theorie. Diese teilt sich wiederum in die Politische Philosophie und Ideengeschichte auf. Die Politische Philosophie ist normativ orientiert und bezieht sich auf die Gegenwart. Ideengeschichtliche Forschungsinteressen hingegen suchen nach geschichtlichen Konzepten, welche für die heutige Zeit von Bedeutung sein können. Die wissenschaftliche Erforschung der systematischen Beschäftigung mit politischen Fragen wird also im Teilbereich Politische Ideengeschichte geleistet. Bei der Politischen Ideengeschichte geht es folglich um „sämtliche Ideen, die sich in irgendeiner Form auf die Politik beziehen, sei es, dass in Form von Utopien, Ideologien oder Literatur [...] der ideale Staat o.ä. beschworen wird, in Form von Pamphleten, Handzetteln, Bildern oder Filmen zu politischen Aktionen aufgerufen wird, in literarischer oder karikierender Weise Kritik an Politik und Politikern geübt wird, in empirisch-theoretischer Form politikwissenschaftliche Erklärungen versucht oder in analytischer Form politische Konstrukte entwickelt werden."[9] Das Forschungsinteresse der Politischen Ideengeschichte liegt also in der Suche

---

[8] Vgl. zu dieser Systematisierung Druwe, U., Politische Theorie, S. 10 ff.
[9] Druwe, U., Politische Theorie, S. 46

nach geschichtlichen und politischen Konzepten, welche auch heute noch als Argumentationsmuster in verschiedenen Zusammenhängen dienen können. Normativ-ontologisch kann man so gute bzw. gerechte Ordnungen begründen. Aus kritisch-dialektischer Warte heraus lässt sich historisch fundierte Kritik an Ideologien und Gesellschaftsordnungen üben. Via empirisch-analytischem Wissenschaftsansatz lassen sich wissenschaftlich begründete bzw. rationale Diskurse über Gegenwartsorientierungen führen.

Politische Ideen innerhalb der Politischen Ideengeschichte stellen Leitgedanken dar, welche Konzeptionen politischer Wirklichkeit für die Gegenwart und Zukunft modellieren. So stellt sich die Frage, welche Politikkonzepte in der Vergangenheit entwickelt wurden. Ein Antwortbeispiel wäre der Rechtsstaat nach Montesquieu. In einem weiteren Schritt kann man nach der Gegenwartsbedeutung der in der Vergangenheit entwickelten Politikkonzepte suchen. Bei Montesquieu könnte eine Antwort lauten, dass das Gewaltenteilungsprinzip bis heute ein wesentliches Merkmal des demokratischen Rechtsstaats darstellt.

Politische Ideengeschichte kann darüber hinaus aus historischer Perspektive der Legitimierung bestehender Ordnungen, Wertorientierungen oder bestimmter Policies dienen. So lässt sich beispielsweise fragen, ob und wie der „Große Lauschangriff" nach Hobbes oder Locke zu rechtfertigen wäre. Mit Hobbes ist es ein leichtes, den „Großen Lauschangriff" zu rechtfertigen. Locke hingegen widerspricht mit seiner liberalen Grundintention vehement dem Eindringen in die Privatsphäre. Internationale politische Verhältnisse, wie die in Kolumbien, kann man durch die Anwendung von Hobbes' Theorie des Naturzustands und Vertragsschlusses illustrieren und erklären.

Als weitere, ausgesuchte Ziele der Politischen Ideengeschichte bzw. der Staatstheorien gelten:[10]

- Politische Urteilskraft und politische Beteiligung in der Bürgerschaft setzen Wissen über die Demokratie voraus.

- Dazu gehören Kenntnisse über die Ideengeschichte, die strukturellen Grundlagen und die Funktionsbedingungen der Demokratie.

- Heutige, moderne Theorie wurde mit Hilfe von Theorien realisiert, in ihr wurden politisch-historische Ideen selektiert und materialisiert.

- Wichtig sind Funktionsbedingungen, der Sinn und der Wert der Demokratie.

- Beschäftigung mit Demokratietheorien von der Antike bis zur Gegenwart kann erhebliche Erklärungsleistungen für die Demokratie der Gegenwart erbringen.

- Bestehende Ordnungen sind geronnene theoretische Ordnungsentwürfe, aufgebaut auf bestimmten Legitimationsmustern.

---

[10] Vgl. zum Folgenden v.a. Politik und Unterricht, Staatstheorien und Massing, P./Breit, G., Vorwort, S. 7-10

- In Geschichte und Politik ist keine Frage endgültig verloren gegangen.
- Die Entschlüsselung der historischen „Denkspuren" bietet die Möglichkeit, Demokratie besser zu verstehen.
- Exemplarische Auseinandersetzung mit Grundtypen politischen Denkens.
- Verdeutlichung des Zusammenhangs zwischen Menschenbildern, der Begründung des Staats und den Aufgaben des Staates.
- Kennen lernen der historisch-kulturellen Kontexte der Politischen Theorien und Verständnis der Zeitepochen.
- Verstehen der Begründung der staatlichen Gewalt.
- Analyse vom Sinn und Wesen des Staates.
- Verstehen des Verhältnisses von Staat und Individuen.
- Reflexion des Ursprungs und der Legitimation staatlicher Autorität.
- Verstehen, wie staatliche Gewalt begründet werden kann.
- Vermittlung demokratischen Grundwissens als Werbung für die repräsentative Demokratie.

- Frage der idealen Organisationsform des Staats und seiner institutionellen Ausprägungen.
- Frage der Maxime politischen Handelns und der sie begründenden Werte und Normen.
- Sinn, Zweck und Mittel der Politik versus Menschenbild.
- Historizität der Denkmodelle politischer Theorie als Deutungs- und Interpretationsmuster zum Verständnis moderner politischer Ordnungssysteme.
- Metareflexion staatsbürgerlicher Erziehung.
- Stabilität der Demokratie hängt davon ab, dass der Bürger die Demokratie und seine eigene Rolle versteht.

Bei den Vertragstheorien, welche eine Spezifikation der Staatstheorien darstellen, geht es darum, theoretisch fundiert zu zeigen, wie aus anthropologischen Prämissen ein Naturzustand abgeleitet wird, welcher die Notwendigkeit eines Vertragsschlusses zur Etablierung einer Gesellschaft und eines Staatswesens begründet.

## 2. Gemeinsamkeiten der Vertragstheorien

Hauptziel der Vertragstheoretiker ist die Legitimierung und Etablierung staatlicher Herrschaft.[11] Die staatliche Herrschaft soll dadurch gerechtfertigt werden, dass alle unter dieser staatlichen Herrschaft lebenden Menschen als Freie und Gleiche der staatlichen Herrschaft durch einen Vertrag zugestimmt haben. Theoretisch muss die erneute Zustimmung zu der gewählten Herrschaftsart und -form immer wieder aufs Neue erfolgen können.[12] Alle Vertragstheorien können sich daher als Möglichkeit einer beliebig wiederholbaren Neuschöpfung des politischen Universums verstehen.[13] Zunächst wird in den verschiedenen Vertragstheorien ein bestimmtes Menschenbild skizziert. Diese anthropologischen Prämissen sind für die weiteren Schlussfolgerungen bis zur Staatskonstitution bestimmend.[14]

Nach den das Individuum betreffenden Überlegungen werden von den Vertragstheoretikern die Menschheit betreffende Szenarien entworfen: Menschen treffen aufeinander und befinden sich in einem Zustand des zumeist asozialen Miteinanders, welches insbesondere durch die Bedingungen einer materiellen Ressourcenknappheit bestimmt wird. Dieses menschliche Zusammenleben in dem Ur-

---

[11] M. Forsyth, Hobbes's contractarianism, S. 37
[12] K.G. Ballestrem, Vertragstheoretische Ansätze in der politischen Philosophie, S. 4
[13] L. Siep, Vertragstheorie, S. 130
[14] M. Dießelhorst, Nachwort, S. 310

bzw. Naturzustand titulierten Szenario ist nicht per se erstrebenswert. Konkurrenz- und Verteilungskämpfe um knappe Ressourcen, Ungewissheit und Unberechenbarkeit gefährden das menschliche (Über-) Leben. Dem Individuum wohnt ein unveräußerlicher Selbsterhaltungstrieb inne. Die Selbsterhaltung an sich wird jedoch durch die Gegebenheiten des Naturzustands gefährdet.

Der Selbsterhaltungstrieb ist eine höchste Priorität besitzende menschliche bzw. dem Menschen a priori immanente Eigenschaft. Um den menschlichen Trieb zum Überleben bei jedem gleichermaßen gewährleisten zu können, wird versucht, in ein „System der Kooperation einzutreten".[15] Dazu ist ein Vertragsschluss nötig. Der Wille, den Vertrag abzuschließen, basiert somit auf nutzenmaximierendem Denken bzw. ökonomischer Rationalität.[16]

Durch den Vertragsschluss wird Herrschaft konstituiert. Dabei ist der Vertrag Legitimationsfaktor für die gegründete Form der Herrschaft. Die Herrschaftsformen und -arten können unterschiedlicher Ausprägung sein. Zusammengefasst handelt es sich in den Werken der Kontraktualisten um vier verschiedene Bestandteile:

Es wird ein Menschenbild entworfen.

Das Menschenbild wirkt sich auf die Art des Naturzustandes aus.

---

[15] K.G. Ballestrem, Vertragstheoretische Ansätze in der politischen Philosophie, S. 11
[16] W. Kersting, Die politische Philosophie des Gesellschaftsvertrags, S. 54

Aus diesem bedrohlichen Naturzustand rettet sich der Mensch durch einen Vertragsabschluss.

Der Vertragsabschluss konstituiert Herrschaftsform und Herrschaftsart.

Die konkrete Ausgestaltung des Staats (Gruppe 2) umfasst nun ihrerseits die sich aus der Notwendigkeit des Staats ergebenden Staatsziele. Die zentrale Frage aus dieser Perspektive lautet, wie der Staat organisiert ist. Von besonderer Wichtigkeit ist der Aspekt, wer der Inhaber der staatlichen Gewalt sein soll. Hinzu kommt die Problematik der Gewaltenteilung. Soll die Staatsgewalt in einer Hand liegen oder ist ein austariertes System von checks und balances notwendig? Eine Grundeinsicht lautet, dass die Staatstheoretiker die Beschaffenheit des Staats aus den anthropologischen Prämissen und dem damit verbundenen Naturzustand ableiten. So verleitet Hobbes' pessimistisches Menschenbild dazu, die staatliche Gewalt in die Hand eines Souveräns zu legen, welcher zugleich kein Mitglied des Vertragsschlusses ist und somit keinen Restriktionen unterliegt. Locke und Montesquieu hingegen insistieren darauf, dass die Staatsgewalt geteilt sein soll und sich in mehreren Händen befindet. Rousseaus Identitätsdemokratie scheint aus verschiedenen Aspekten bedenklich: „Gerade weil sie den Gedanken der Demokratie usupiert, halte ich sie für außerordentlich gefährlich; denn sie trifft auf den von Fraenkel so genannten weit verbreiteten Vulgärdemokratismus und findet daher, wie man allenthalben beobachten kann, viele Anhänger unter idealistischen Demokraten. Die Durchsetzung einer realistischeren Demokratietheorie ist daher eine Lebensfrage für unsere freiheitliche Ordnung."[17] Hobbes und Rousseau bilden folglich das extreme Spektrum der Staatstheorien zur Zeit der Aufklärung ab, während Locke und Montesquieu bis heute als Vorbilder gelten. Aus demokratietheoretischer Perspektive ist die Frage der Staatsform zentral. In der Epoche der Aufklärung finden sich die Vorläufer unserer heutigen westlichen Demokratien. So ist beispielsweise bereits bei Montesquieu ein differenziertes Gewaltenteilungssystem angelegt, welches sich heute in zahlreichen westlichen Demokratien in nuce findet.

---

[17] Sutor, B., Didaktik des politischen Unterrichts, S. 111

## 3. Die Epoche der Aufklärung als Wiege der Demokratie

Es ist nicht möglich, hier die gesamte Zeitspanne der Aufklärung (17. und 18. Jahrhundert) und die räumlichen Besonderheiten ganz Europas zu berücksichtigen. Die folgenden Ausführungen beziehen sich auf die ganze Epoche der Aufklärung und v.a. die Entwicklung in Deutschland.

Die geistesgeschichtliche Fundierung der demokratisch orientierten Staatstheorien liegt in der Epoche der Aufklärung. Unser heutiges Herrschafts- und Gesellschaftssystem wird durch in der Epoche der Aufklärung entstandene Merkmale wie Gewaltenkontrolle, Repräsentationsprinzip u.ä. gekennzeichnet. Darüber hinaus finden sich zahlreiche weitere Strukturelemente moderner Demokratien bereits in Staatstheorien zur Zeit der Aufklärung. Die westlichen Demokratien sind somit als Kind der Aufklärung zu betrachten. Insofern ist es wichtig, bei einer ideengeschichtlichen Auseinandersetzung mit demokratischen Staatstheorien die Epoche der Aufklärung mit in die Analyse einzubeziehen. Im Folgenden werden demnach einige der wichtigsten Entwicklungsmerkmale der Epoche der Aufklärung aufgezählt. Dabei handelt es sich um Entwicklungen und Tendenzen aus dem gesellschaftlichen, ökonomischen, pädagogischen und politischen System.

## 3.1 Soziopolitische Merkmale der Aufklärung

Es ist ein zentrales Merkmal der Aufklärung, dass sie nach der Lebenssituation des Menschen in seiner vorgefundenen Umwelt fragt.[18] Die Aufklärung besaß tendenziell einen antifeudalen und antireligiösen Charakter. Abstrakt kann man den Vorgang sozialer Differenzierung im 18. Jahrhundert auf die Formel des Übergangs von stratifikatorischer (ständischer) Schichtung zu funktionaler Differenzierung beschreiben.[19] Was Aufklärung oder Fortschritt heißt, löst die alten Ordnungen radikal auf.[20]

In der Aufklärung gab es eine Steigerung der Rationalität, Organisation und Verwissenschaftlichung. Zudem ersetzte die Rechtsgleichheit ständisch-korporative Herrschaftsbeziehungen. Individualisierung und Rollentrennung sind Folgen der funktionalen Differenzierung, welche das Individuum betreffen. Die räumliche, soziale und kulturelle Mobilität erhöhte sich. Durch die Einbeziehung der Wissenschaften konnte in der Landwirtschaft die Umstellung von der Subsistenzwirtschaft zur kommerziellen Produktion landwirtschaftlicher Güter erfolgen. Es war die soziale Differenzierung im 18. Jahrhundert, welche die Entwicklung des bürgerlichen Individuums ermöglichte. Als Wegbereiter gelten der

---

[18] Kaiser, G. Aufklärung, Empfindsamkeit, Sturm und Drang, S. 18.

[19] Vgl. zu den folgenden Ausführungen Schmidt, S., Die Selbstorganisation des Sozialsystems Literatur im 18. Jahrhundert. Frankfurt am Main 1989, S. 65-198.

[20] Luhmann, N., Die Gesellschaft der Gesellschaft. Band 2. Frankfurt am Main 1997, S. 734.

Pietismus, die Säkularisierung der politischen Ordnung und die rechtliche Emanzipation.

Produktive Arbeit verbindet sich über den Geldmechanismus mit der Wirtschaft, Fähigkeiten und Persönlichkeitsaspekte sind zunehmend im ökonomischen Prozess von Bedeutung. Arbeitsteilung bedingt die Entwicklung sozialer Rollen und die Unterscheidung zwischen Rolle und Person. In der durch soziale Rollen organisierten Gesellschaft kann jeder Bürger Zugang zu allen gesellschaftlichen Funktionen erhalten. Unter dem Gleichheitspostulat werden die allgemeine Rechts- und Geschäftsfähigkeit unter der Aufhebung ständischer Schranken, die Demokratisierung des politischen Lebens, die Realisierung der allgemeinen Schulpflicht und die vollständige Monetarisierung der Wirtschaft subsumiert.

Die kapitalistische Freiheit der Konkurrenz bildet das ideologische Fundament des neuen Individualismus. Kapitalismus strebt nach monetärem Gewinn und basiert auf freier Arbeit. Zudem setzte sich im 18. Jahrhundert der Entwicklungsgedanke durch. In der Transzendentalphilosophie erreicht die theoretische Konzeptualisierung des Menschen ihren Kulminationspunkt. Zeit spielte als individuelle und gesellschaftliche Komponente eine zentrale Rolle. Damit einher geht z.B. der Aspekt der Leistungssteigerung in der Wirtschaft. Das Menschliche des eigenen Subjekts wird kultiviert und das menschliche Gefühl verabsolutiert.

Mit der gesellschaftlichen Differenzierung und dem damit verbundenen Risiko gestiegener Selektionszwänge steigen die Risiken für das Individuum. Als perfektibles Wesen wird der Mensch zur letzten Legitimationsbasis seiner selbst. Freundschaft bildet ein wesentliches Konzept zur Selbstverwirklichung des Individuums. Durch die Verfügung über Privateigentum und die Teilnahme am Tauschverkehr realisiert sich die Autonomie der Privatleute in der Familie. Merkmale der Familie sind der freie Einzelne, dauerhafte Liebesbeziehungen und die zweckfreie Entfaltung aller Fähigkeiten der Familienmitglieder. Liebe und Sexualität besitzen gesellschaftliche Relevanz, werden jedoch nicht zuletzt auf Grund von Krankheiten und anderen moralisch-ethischen Überlegungen als problematisch verstanden. Zweck der in der politischen Ordnung frei gegebenen Wirtschaftsordnung sind die Entwicklung von Kultur und Wohlstand. Dies bedingt zugleich die Idee der gesellschaftlichen Evolution in der bürgerlichen Gesellschaft. Bildung und Kultur können die Wildheit des Einzelmenschen zu Gunsten der Menschheit bändigen.[21]

Staat und Gesellschaft in der Aufklärung sind noch nicht vollständig voneinander getrennt, befinden sich aber im Trennungsprozess. Zentral ist, dass sich der so skizzierte gesellschaftliche Prozess auf der Basis der Vernunft vollzog, welche zugleich einen Rechts- und Machtanspruch in der Öffentlichkeit anmeldete. Die Gesellschaftstheorie der Aufklärung agiert zunehmend in strukturellen Dimensionen.

---

[21] Meyer-Drawe, K., Kulturwissenschaftliche Pädagogik, S. 605.

## 3.2 Aufklärung und Bildung

Seit dem Ende der 1790er möchte eine bestimmte gesellschaftliche Schicht ihre Individualisierungschancen via dem Instrumentarium Bildung nutzen. Bildung an sich wird hingegen angeblich zweckfrei. Unter dem Stichwort des „pädagogischen Jahrhunderts" finden sich die Alphabetisierungsmaßnahmen, die Ausweitung der Schulpflicht und der Mädchenerziehung.

Die pädagogische Semantik der Aufklärung korrellierte mit gesellschaftlichen Entwicklungen:

„Im 18. Jahrhundert wird dieser alteuropäische Humanismus durch einen Neuhumanismus ersetzt, der von sozialer Stratifikation abstrahiert und sich auf <<Subjekte>> schlechthin bezieht. Dem entspricht die Ersetzung des Begriffs der (naturalen) Perfektion durch den Begriff der Bildung."[22]

Die Erziehung soll den Menschen als gesellschaftliches Wesen mit einer inneren, frei akzeptierten Form ausstatten, welche zugleich die gesellschaftlichen Verhältnisse humanisiert. Ein weiteres Kalkül liegt in der Vermutung, dass die Bildung den Menschen ungefährlich macht und ihn entwaffnet. Kurzzeitig fand in der Pädagogik eine Begeisterung für transzendentaltheoretische Ideen statt. Es wurde aber bald erkannt, dass, abgesehen von Kant, weder methodisch noch institutionell Hilfe von dieser Seite zu erwarten war. Individualität und selbst-

---

[22] Luhmann, N. Das Erziehungssystem der Gesellschaft, S. 17 f.

gesetzte Lebensziele wurden akzeptiert und gefördert. Aufgabe der zunehmend in die Autonomie getriebenen, d.h. ausdifferenzierten Pädagogik war für die strukturelle Kompatibilität von Mensch und Gesellschaft zu sorgen.

Die Lehre des 18. Jahrhunderts betont die Offenheit des Menschen, der auf Gesellschaft, Milieu, Kultur etc. angewiesen ist. Die Perfektibilität des Menschen, d.h. seine Unfertigkeit, ist wesentliches Merkmal der Pädagogik des 18. Jahrhunderts. Als nicht bestimmtes Wesen nimmt das Kind auf, was ihm zur Selbstbestimmung geboten wird. Der Erzieher soll das Kind denaturieren, es primär als erlebendes und dann erst als handelndes Wesen sehen. Rationalität, Kultur und Perfektibilität lautet die sich herausbildende pädagogische Semantik des 18. Jahrhunderts. Durch die Einführung des allgemeinen Schulwesens wird die Schule zur Dirigierungsstelle für Chancen des späteren Leben. Die skizzierte Entwicklung hat zur Frage geführt, warum der Staat Karriereinteressen finanzieren sollte. Als Organisation des politischen Systems kann der Staat nicht selber erziehen. Deshalb finanziert er aus Steuermitteln die Kosten von Schulen. Damit einher geht die Professionalisierung des Erziehungswesens, mit eigens für den erziehenden Unterricht ausgebildeten Lehrkräften.

## 4. Hobbes' Staatstheorie

### 4.1 Biographischer und historischer Kontext

Thomas Hobbes wurde 1588 als Vikarssohn in Wiltshire geboren und er starb 1679 in Hardwick. Seine akademische Karriere ging zügig vonstatten; manche hielten ihn für ein Wunderkind, da er mit vier Jahren lesen und schreiben konnte. Bereits 1607, also mit 19 Jahren, erwarb er das Recht, an der Universität Vorlesungen über Logik abhalten zu können. Später wurde Hobbes in Paris Lehrer des späteren Königs Karl II.[23]

Der englische Bürgerkrieg (1642-1649), in welchem der puritanische Heerführer Oliver Cromwell (1599-1658) mit der Parlamentspartei gegen den katholischen Stuartkönig Karl I. (1625-1649) kämpfte, sowie die aus dem Bürgerkrieg hervorgehende Republik des Commonwealth waren prägende Ereignisse für das staatsphilosophische Verständnis von Hobbes. Da er für die Seite der Krone eintrat und diese in der Auseinandersetzung unterlag, musste er 1640 nach Frankreich fliehen. Elf Jahre später erschien der "Leviathan" in englischer Sprache. 1668 erschien der "Leviathan" erneut, aber diesmal in lateinischer Sprache und mit Modifizierungen, d.h. Abschwächungen im religiösen Bereich.

Hobbes' Erfahrungen während des Bürgerkrieges, schließlich die Enthauptung Karls I. und das Com-

---

[23] Politik und Unterricht. Zeitschrift zur Gestaltung des politischen Unterrichts, S. 6

monwealth unter der Diktatur Cromwells bestimmten in großem Ausmaß die Konzeption des Buches "Leviathan": Es "drängte sich der Friedensgedanke als Postulat an seine Realisierbarkeit auf; gleichzeitig deduzierte H. durch seine Analyse des Menschen und seiner gesellschaftlichen Existenz die Unmöglichkeit eines Friedens."[24] Dieses Diktum zum Frieden wurde durch die mathematische und mechanistische Methodik begründet.[25]

Es ist ersichtlich, dass Hobbes' Reflexionen realhistorischer Geschehnisse ihren Niederschlag in seinem philosophischen Werke fanden. Der Wunsch nach Frieden war bei ihm so stark vorhanden, dass er die scholastische Tradition der Wahrheitssuche hinter sich ließ und statt dessen das Primat des Friedens postulierte.

## 4.2 Menschenbild, Naturzustand und Vertragsabschluss

Der natürliche Mensch zeichnet sich bei Hobbes durch Willensunfreiheit aus, der Handlungsgrundantrieb sind Furcht und Selbsterhaltung.[26] Er besitzt Vernunft i.S.v. Zweckrationalität und kann Ursache- / Wirkungszusammenhänge identifizieren.[27] Das Zusammenspiel von Mensch und Naturzustand zeichnet sich durch ressourcenbedingte Konkurrenz, darin implizierter Verfeindung und gewaltan-

---

[24] Schneider, T., Hobbes, S. 396.
[25] Druwe, U., Politische Theorie, S. 128.
[26] Schneider, T., Hobbes, S. 397
[27] T. Hobbes, Leviathan, S. 44

wendender Gewaltprävention aus. Im Naturrecht herrschen Gleichheit der Menschen, ferner Selbsterhaltungsrecht, Friedens- und Vertragseinhaltungspflicht etc.

Im Naturzustand versucht der Stärkere sich gegen Schwächere durchzusetzen. Alle Menschen laufen ständig Gefahr, an Leib und Leben bedroht zu werden, da es keine Sanktionsinstanz gibt, welche das Zusammenleben im Naturzustand reguliert. Folglich wird die Frage der Geltungsgewissheit bedeutsam. Die Vernunft bzw. Kooperationsrationalität[28] bestimmt also die Institutionalisierung einer machtgestützten Ordnung, die qua Herrschaftsvertrag (als Gesellschaftsvertrag (jeder Mensch mit jedem zur bürgerlichen Gesellschaftskonstituierung) und Unterwerfungsvertrag (Entäußerung der gesellschaftsvertraglich konstituierten Rechtspersönlichkeit zur Etablierung des Staates)) konstituiert wird. Daraus resultiert der inneren und äußeren Frieden - mit ungeteilter Macht (Gewaltmonopol) - zu garantierende Leviathan. Er ist Garant, aber nicht Unterworfener der Rechtsordnung,[29] welche sich durch die bürgerlichen Gesetze als staatlich garantierte Naturrechte auszeichnet.

Kann deren Einhaltung durch den Staat nicht garantiert werden, so gibt es ein individuelles Widerstandsrecht, welches zur Anarchie (Naturzustand) führen kann. Bürgerliche Freiheit existiert nur da,

---

[28] Kersting, W., Thomas Hobbes zur Einführung, S. 118
[29] Speth spricht von einem Rechtsverzicht zugunsten des Leviathan, in Speth, R., Thomas Hobbes, S. 97

wo es keine Gesetze gibt. Die analytisch zu interpretierenden Elemente des natürlichen Menschen, Naturzustands und Naturrechts sind Modellelemente zur Begründung staatlicher Ordnung. Die Eigenschaften des Modellmenschen bedingen den Herrschaftsvertrag. Der Staat hat Ordnung und Sicherheit durch Rechtsetzung zu garantieren, weshalb er ein ungeteiltes Gewaltmonopol besitzt.

## 4.3 Nach Vertragsschluss: Der Staat

Hobbes beschreibt im 19. Kapitel des "Leviathan", wie der von ihm kreierte Staat aussehen könnte. Seine Staatsphilosophie wendet sich, nachdem Art und Weise der Staatsgründung beschrieben wurde, der Frage zu, wie die Staatsform nach dem Vertragsschluss konkret auszusehen hat.

Drei verschiedene mögliche Staatsformen gibt es für Hobbes. Dabei folgt er zumindest im terminologischen Bereich den bereits von Aristoteles entwickelten und beschriebenen Darstellungen: "Deshalb kann es auch nur dreierlei Staatsverfassungen geben, nämlich die monarchische, bei der die höchste Gewalt in den Händen eines einzigen ist; die demokratische, bei der diese Gewalt von einer Versammlung, zu der jeder freien Zutritt hat, ausgeübt wird, und die aristokratische, bei der die höchste Gewalt dem vornehmsten Bürgerstande anvertraut ist." (Lev, S. 167) Der Unterschied in den drei Staatsformen liegt für Hobbes darin, dass die Bürger unterschiedliche Mitwirkungsmöglichkeiten für die Friedenserhaltung haben. (Lev, S. 168)

Dass Hobbes für die Ausformung des Staates die drei verschiedenen Möglichkeiten der Monarchie, der Aristokratie und der Demokratie zugelassen hat, lässt sich sicherlich damit erklären, dass es ihm hauptsächlich auf das instrumentell-funktionale Wirken des Staates ankommt. Allerdings ist deutlich darauf hinzuweisen, dass bei Hobbes der Souverän, egal welcher Ausprägung ein absolutes Machtmonopol besitzt.

## 4.4 Der Souverän und die Untertanen: Vom Zweck des Staats

Unabhängig davon, wie beim Leviathan die konkrete Ausgestaltung vorgenommen wird (Monarchie, Aristokratie, Demokratie); seine Kompetenzen und Befugnisse sind in jedem der drei Fälle gleich. Hinsichtlich der Kompetenzen und Befugnisse richtet Hobbes nunmehr sein Hauptaugenmerk auf Machtbeschränkungen. Hobbes rechtfertigt von vornherein alle möglichen Handlungen des Souveräns und möchte sie gegenüber den Untertanen mit dem Argument unangreifbar machen, dass der Souverän selber ja kein Vertragsmitglied sei. (Lev, S. 158 ff.) Die Staatszwecke sind Frieden und Schutz, und alleine der Souverän kann geeignete Maßnahmen und Mittel zur Erlangung dieser Ziele bestimmen und für ihre Realisierung sorgen. Diese Friedenssorge gilt sowohl für die inneren Beziehungen des Staatswesens als auch für seine äußeren. (Lev, S. 160 f.) Um dies zu gewährleisten, wird dem Souverän eine große Kompetenzfülle eingeräumt.

## 4.5 Organisierung staatlicher Gewalt

Weiterer, wichtiger Punkt staatlicher Kompetenzfülle ist die Legislative. Der Staat ist zur Legislative berechtigt. Hobbes bringt das Recht der Gesetzgebung in den Zusammenhang mit den Eigentumsrechten, welche bei ihm eine wesentliche Rolle für die Selbsterhaltung spielen: Die „höchste Gewalt (hat, S.S.) das Recht, diejenigen Vorschriften zu erlassen, welche das Eigentum betreffen [...] was er (der Untertan, S.S.) mit Recht tun und nicht tun dürfe." (Lev, S. 161)

Ferner vereint der Souverän in Hobbes Staatsmodell auch die Judikative in sich: Es „gehört [...] zur höchsten Gewalt, alle Rechtshändel der Wahrheit und den Rechten nach zu untersuchen und alle Streitigkeiten zu entscheiden, mit einem Worte: das *Richteramt.*" (Lev, S. 162) Hobbes begründet die Rechtsprechung durch die höchste Gewalt weiter damit, dass die Bürger ohne "Richteramt" vor Unrecht nicht gesichert seien und sich wegen Eigentumsstreitigkeiten ansonsten in dem Zustand des Krieges aller gegen alle befänden. (Lev, S. 162) Zur Judikative und Legislative kommt der Aspekt der ausführenden Gewalt hinzu. Der Souverän vereint auch die Exekutive in sich. Der ausführenden Gewalt misst Hobbes die größte und höchste Bedeutung zu, da er sie als relevantesten Faktor für die Innen- und Außenstabilisierung des Staates ansieht: Die „höchste Gewalt (muss, S.S.) Krieg gegen andere Staaten nach Gutdünken beschließen oder Frieden mit ihnen machen [...] Denn der Schutz der

Bürger hängt von den Kriegsheeren ab, die Stärke dieser von der Einigkeit des Staates und diese allein von der Person des Oberherrn. Das Recht über die Kriegsheere ist schon an und für sich die höchste Gewalt, weil darin die ganze Stärke des Staates besteht." (Lev, S. 162)

Es ist unschwer zu erkennen, dass der Souverän in Hobbes' Staatskonstruktion eine große Machtfülle in sich vereinigt. Die Bürger geben alle gleichermaßen ihre Rechte und ihre Macht auf und übertragen diese der höchsten Gewalt. Sie üben einen einseitigen Rechtsverzicht. Die Untertänigkeit gegenüber dem Souverän ist ein wichtiges Merkmal in der Theorie von Hobbes. Kausalgründe für diesen Rechtsverzicht waren das dualistische Menschenbild, das Szenario des Naturzustands und die Hoffnung auf ein Leben in Frieden und Sicherheit. Gegen den Souverän selber kann man keine Rechtsansprüche geltend machen. Man kann nur darauf hinweisen, dass er eine Funktionalität hinsichtlich der inneren wie äußeren Friedenssicherung, der Lebenserhaltung der Individuen und der Möglichkeit von Eigentumserwerb und Eigentumsakkumulation besitzt.

Man könnte hinsichtlich der Machtfülle des Souveräns von absoluter Herrschaft sprechen und davon, "dass absolute Herrschaft nicht nur eine hinreichende Bedingung, sondern auch eine notwendige Bedingung für die Beendigung des Kriegszustandes und die Errichtung einer friedlichen Koexistenzordnung ist."[30]

Aus dem bisher Genannten kann man als Extremableitung folgern, dass es in Hobbes' Modell zwischen der absoluten Herrschaft eines Souveräns und einer Anarchie im Naturzustand keinen Mittelweg gibt. Entweder es herrscht ein Krieg aller gegen alle oder der höchsten Gewalt sind alle Bürger gleichermaßen untertan. Der Leviathan soll den Menschen die Selbsterhaltung garantieren, den Eigentumserwerb ermöglichen und sie vor der Macht anderer Leviathane schützen.

---

[30] Kersting, W., Die politische Philosophie des Gesellschaftsvertrages, S. 100.

# 5. Lockes Staatstheorie

## 5.1 Biographischer und historischer Kontext

Einer der bis heute für das westliche Politik- und Staatsverständnis wichtigsten Theoretiker ist John Locke. Er lebte von 1632 bis 1704. Locke studierte in Oxford mit dem Schwerpunkt auf empirischen Fächern wie Medizin und Naturwissenschaften. 1667 wurde John Locke zum Arzt des Earl of Shaftesbury bestellt. Durch diesen wurde er vermutlich auch dazu angeregt, sich auf ökonomische und politische Studien zu konzentrieren. Diese Studien beschäftigten sich v.a. mit den Aspekten Geld und Eigentum. Nicht umsonst gilt John Locke als zentraler Ahnherr des Liberalismus und Wegbereiter moderner, liberalistischer Politik- und Wirtschaftskonzeptionen.

Im Zusammenhang mit dem Aufstieg der Shaftesburys erhielt John Locke auch unterschiedliche politische Ämter. Mit Shaftesbury musste Locke fliehen, kehrte aber nach der „Glorreichen Revolution", der Restauration der Stuarts 1660 und damit der endgültigen Niederlage des Commonwealth, 1688 nach England zurück. Trotz der real-historischen „Glorreichen Revolution" und den „Bill of Rights" musste es ein zentrales Anliegen von Locke sein, die Rechte der Bevölkerung und des Parlaments theoretisch zu sichern und zu modellieren.

Ein Jahr später, also 1689, veröffentlichte er sein politiktheoretisches Hauptwerk, die „Two Treaties of Government". Die Begründung einer funktionierenden politischen Ordnung kann als Lockes zentrales politiktheoretisches Problem angesehen werden. Es ist der Ausgewogenheit von Lockes Argumentation zuzuschreiben, welche die Freiheit sowohl gebietet und sie zugleich zügelt, welche ihm große Beachtung einbringt. Lockes Schriften beeinflussten in hohem Maße realpolitische Vorgänge. So rekurrierten die amerikanischen Patrioten des amerikanischen Unabhängigkeitskriegs in großem Maß auf die Theorien John Lockes.

John Locke wird als jüngerer Zeitgenosse von Thomas Hobbes angesehen: „In der Tat weisen zahlreiche Stellen in seinem politischen Hauptwerk, den „Treaties of Government", darauf hin, das er bestrebt war, den „Leviathan" zu widerlegen."[31]

Bei John Locke (2. Hälfte des 17. Jahrhunderts) ist historisch-kontextuell zu berücksichtigen, dass sich das feudal-agrarische ständische hin zum bürgerlich-kapitalistischen Weltbild entwickelte bzw. die Wirtschaftsform änderte sich von der Substitutions- zur Marktwirtschaft. Nicht zuletzt im Gefolge der beginnenden Aufklärung wurde der Standesangehörige zum autonomen Individuum.

John Locke wird das Verdienst zugeschrieben, in jeglicher Hinsicht bahnbrechend für die europäische Aufklärung gewesen zu sein.[32] Des Weiteren ist kontextuell die rationalistische Naturrechtslehre zu würdigen, was die Säkularisierung ehemals dem

---

[31] Politik und Unterricht. Zeitschrift zur Gestaltung des politischen Unterrichts, S. 6
[32] Schneider, T., Locke, S. 512

transzendenten Bereich anheim fallender Staatskonzeptionen bedeutet.

In Lockes Modell wird empirisch Gegebenes mit induktiv Wahrgenommenem und rational Verarbeitetem und damit Erkanntem gleichgesetzt.[33] D.h., dass Locke seine Aussagen über den Naturzustand etc. als empirische Aussagen auffasst. Im rekonstruierten Modell ist seine Begründung einer funktionierenden politischen Ordnung aber als analytischer Begriffs- und Aussagenzusammenhang zu interpretieren. Ernsthaft kann nämlich nicht von einem empirischen Menschenbild, Urvertrag etc. ausgegangen werden.

## 5.2 Menschenbild und Naturzustand

Lockes anthropologische Konstruktprämissen lauten, dass der natürliche Mensch vernunftbegabt und sozial, frei und gleich ist. Der Modellmensch verfährt lebenserhaltend, nutzenmaximierend und eigentumsakkumulierend und geht zu dieser Zielrealisierung einen Gesellschaftsvertrag ein. Hinzu kommt, dass der Mensch Güter aneignend und diese anhäufend verfährt. Bereits aus der Anthropologie heraus wird die liberalistische Eigentumstheorie bei Locke evident.

Im Naturzustand herrscht vollkommene Freiheit, wobei jeder in eigener Sache zum Richter werden kann. Die Freiheit bedeutet aber nicht automatisch

---

[33] Vgl. eine ähnliche Argumentation bei Druwe, U., Studienführer Politikwissenschaft, S. 145

Zügellosigkeit, denn die Menschen folgen dem Naturgesetz, wonach niemand einem anderen Schaden zufügen soll. Naturaneignung und die Bearbeitung der Natur darf nur zum Eigengebrauch und eigenem Konsum vollzogen werden.

Durch die Einführung des Geldes allerdings kann die Akkumulation über den Eigenbedarf hinausgehen. Das ruft Neid und daraus resultierende Bedrohung und Konflikte auf den Plan. Diese Tatsache erfordert neue Aneignungs- und Eigentumsregeln. Zentrales Problem hierbei ist, dass kein Gewaltmonopol und folglich auch keine Sanktionsinstanz vorhanden ist, also eine Suboptimalität hinsichtlich des Schutzes von Eigentum und Leben im Naturzustand zu verzeichnen ist.[34] Es mangelt folglich an allgemein verbindlichen Normen. Das Naturrecht impliziert bei Locke das zentrale Selbsterhaltungsrecht. Letzteres ist im besitzindividualistischen Sinne zu verstehen, da darunter das Recht auf Leben, Besitz und Eigentum zu subsumieren ist.

## 5.3 Vertragsabschluss

Des Weiteren besteht bei Locke die Pflicht zur Erhaltung der Anderen und der Einhaltung von Aneignungs- und Eigentumsregeln. Daraus folgt eine notwendige Institutionalisierung einer Leben und Eigentum schützenden Ordnung. Dies ist der eigentliche und primäre Staatszweck in Lockes politiktheoretischer Konzeption.

---

[34] Speth, R., John Locke, S. 103

Der politische Körper entsteht dann durch den freiwilligen Zusammenschluss im Urvertrag aus einer Kette wechselseitiger Verträge oder bei nachfolgenden Generationen im impliziten Vertrag nach dem Prinzip der stillschweigenden Zustimmung.

## 5.4 Ziel der Staatsbildung

In der politischen Gemeinschaft lenkt die größte Kraft den (Staats-) Körper nach dem Mehrheitsprinzip (consent). Die Gewalten werden idealtypischer Weise zwischen dem Besitzbürgertum als Legislative und der Krone als Exekutive geteilt. Dies soll die Dominanz einer gesellschaftlichen Macht über die anderen solchen verhindern. Die Legislative besitzt die Aufgabe, das Naturrecht in positives Recht zum Lebens- und Eigentumsschutz umzuwandeln.

Die Gewalten sind Machttreuhänder (trust). Wird Macht fehlgeleitet oder missbraucht, so besteht das Widerstandsrecht bzw. das Recht auf Emigration. Im Gegensatz zu Hobbes spielt die Aufrechterhaltung der individuellen Freiheit im Staatsgebilde bei Locke eine zentrale Rolle. Der Staat besitzt die Funktion, Leben und Eigentum durch positives Recht zu schützen. Im Staat soll der Kriegszustand vermieden werden. Der Staat soll die persönliche Freiheit der Untertanen ebenso wie Ihr Eigentum in Frieden und Sicherheit schützen.

## 5.5 Organisierung der staatlichen Gewalt und Staatsform

Eine bis heute relevante Besonderheit ist bei John Locke das qua checks und balances austarierte Gewaltmonopol. Für die Bildung der politischen Gemeinschaft bestehen nach Locke mehrere Möglichkeiten. Falls sich die politische Macht in Form der Legislative in den Händen der Mehrheit befindet, dann handelt es sich um eine demokratische Regierungsform. Herrscht nur einer, dann handelt es sich um eine Monarchie, herrscht eine Gruppe von „Politikern", dann handelt es sich um eine Oligarchie.

In Lockes Staatskonzeption existiert die sogenannte föderative Gewalt, welche das Verhalten des Staates nach außen reguliert, denn sie schließt Verträge, entscheidet über Krieg und Frieden u.ä. Neben der föderativen Gewalt ist der König ebenso maßgebend für die exekutive Gewalt, d.h., dass der König die staatliche Gewalt ausüben kann. Der staatlichen Gewalt in persona des Königs werden Grenzen durch die Legislative gesetzt. An deren Gesetzen muss sich der König orientieren und für deren Einhaltung sorgen. Es ist die Aufgabe des Volks die Legislative zu wählen und abzuberufen. Die Legislative ist somit ein wichtiger Bestandteil zur Ausübung der staatlichen Gewalt. Die Exekutive ist bei Locke der Legislative untergeordnet und kann von dieser auch abgesetzt werden, wobei die Exekutive die Legislative einberufen darf.

Ein zentrales Moment, wie die staatliche Gewalt ausgeübt werden kann besteht in mehreren Kontrollmomenten der Staatsgewalt. Dazu gehören die Gewaltenteilung, Gesetze, Wahlen und das Widerstandsrecht bzw. das Recht auf Emigration.

## 5.6 Fazit

Als Fazit kann festgehalten werden:

- Politische Entscheidungsprozesse werden auf Basis des Mehrheitsprinzips gefällt.
- Das Ziel des Staats ist der Schutz der Freiheit und des Eigentums der Individuen.
- Notwendig ist eine Gewaltenteilung zwischen Legislative und Exekutive.
- Souverän ist das Volk, welches Macht an Repräsentanten in regelmäßigen Wahlen delegiert.
- Richter überwachen die Bindung der Gewalten an das Recht (Rechtsstaatsprinzip).
- Es besteht das Recht auf Widerstand oder Emigration, falls Staat Einhaltung der Naturrechte nicht garantieren kann.

# 6. Montesquieus Staatstheorie

## 6.1 Biographischer und historischer Kontext

Der zum französischen Hochadel gehörende Charles de Secondat Montesquieu wurde 1689 auf Schloss La Brède bei Bordeaux geboren und starb 1755 bei Paris. Montesquieu besaß bereits zu Lebzeiten großen Einfluss. Sowohl Progressive als auch Konservative bemühten sich, Montesquieu für sich vereinnahmen zu können. Seit 1727 gehörte Montesquieu der ehrwürdigen Académie francaise an, aber ebenso dem politisch fortschrittlichen Club de l'entresol. Montesquieu studierte alte Sprachen und Rechtswissenschaften. Von 1716 bis 1726 war er Senatspräsident in Bordeaux. Ab 1727 widmete sich Montesquieu seinen literarischen Arbeiten und wissenschaftlichen Studien, welche durch Reisetätigkeiten durch Österreich, Italien, Deutschland und Holland unterstützt wurden. Montesquieus Einfluss machte sogar vor der katholischen Kirche nicht halt. Als Montesquieu „1755 schwer an Grippe erkrankte, am 5. Februar gar ins Koma fiel, ließ sich Papst Benedikt XIV. durch seinen Pariser Nuntius laufend berichten, ob der angesehene Rechtsdenker und Moralphilosoph nicht endlich gebeichtet und seinen Frieden mit der Römischen Kirche gemacht hätte."[35]

Das zentrale Werks Montesquieus ist „Vom Geist der Gesetze" von 1748. In ihm entwickelt er insbesondere im 6. Kapitel des 11. Buches seine Gewal-

---

[35] Hausmann, F.-R., Montesquieu, S. 605

tenteilungslehre, welche bis heute nichts an ihrer Aktualität eingebüßt hat.[36]

## 6.2 Menschenbild

Als eine der zentralen Figuren der europäischen Hochaufklärung postuliert Montesquieu „die Vernunft des Menschen, seine Fähigkeit, den sinnhaften Zusammenhang der Dinge erkennen und eine dementsprechende gute gesellschaftliche und politische Ordnung einrichten zu können."[37] Trotz der Vernunft des Menschen sieht Montesquieu die Gefahr eines Machtmissbrauchs: „Es ist eine immer wieder festzustellende Tatsache, dass jeder Mensch, der Macht hat, auch in Gefahr steht, sie zu missbrauchen; er hält erst damit inne, wenn er auf Widerstand stößt."[38] Somit ist das Menschenbild tendenziell positiv veranlagt, ohne dabei die realen Gefahren zu vernachlässigen.

## 6.3 Geschichtsbild und Sozialstruktur

Montesquieu entstammte dem Adel und er setzte sich auch publizistisch für die Privilegien der Adelsstand ein. Der Adel sollte Theorie immanent bei Montesquieu eine unabhängige Zwischengewalt bilden, welche „die Degeneration der absolutistischen Monarchie in orientalische Despotie bzw. der

---

[36] Politik und Unterricht. Zeitschrift zur Gestaltung des politischen Unterrichts, S. 7
[37] Pesch, V., Charles des Montesquieu, S. 113
[38] Montesquieu, C.d., Vom Geist der Gesetze, S. 53

freiheitlichen Republik der Pöbelherrschaft verhindern sollte."[39] Offensichtlich misstraute Montesquieu sowohl dem monarchischen Herrscher wie auch der Herrschaft des Volkes. Montesquieus Geschichtsbild ist säkularisiert und erforscht die Ursachen des Geschichtsablaufs und der menschlichen Institutionen. Dies entspricht auch Montesquieus Vorstellungen der Sozialstruktur. Diese zergliedert die Gesellschaft in Adel, Monarch und Volk, was mit der von Aristoteles tradierten Staatsformenlehre Aristokratie, Monarchie und Demokratie korrespondiert. Im Gegensatz zu den älteren Staatstheorien ist bei Montesquieu die Kombination der Staatsformen- und Sozialstrukturanalyse neu.

## 6.4 Organisierung staatlicher Gewalt

Das Ziel von Montesquieus Theorie ist es, eine von Gesetzen beherrschte Gemeinschaft zu ermöglichen. Bei Montesquieu korrespondiert die politische Freiheit mit der Vernunft, denn man besitzt die Freiheit das zu tun, was man rational wollen soll. So kann man auch das Verhältnis von Individuum und Staat beschreiben, dass der Staat dem Individuum die Freiheit ermöglicht, das tun zu können, was man tun soll.

Bei Montesquieu verfügt jeder Staat über drei Arten der Gewalt: Über „die Gewalt, Gesetze zu geben, über die Gewalt, die Handlungen zu vollziehen, die in den Bereich des Völkerrechts gehören, und über

---

[39] Hausmann, F.-R., Montesquieu, S. 606

die Gewalt, für die Beobachtung alles dessen zu sorgen, was in das Gebiet des bürgerlichen Rechts fällt."[40] Eine Verfassung, die dies ermöglicht, basiert auf der Teilung der drei zentralen Gewalten:[41]

Die Legislative besitzt die Hoheit über den Staatsetat und kann die Steuergesetze erlassen. Zudem soll sie die Exekutive kontrollieren.

Die Exekutive ist die ausführende Gewalt und hat als administrative Gewalt kein Gesetzesinitiativrecht. Vielmehr ist sie an der Gesetzgebung nur via Vetorecht beteiligt. Das Veto kann allerdings überstimmt werden.

Die Judikative wird aus der Exekutive heraus gelöst und stellt eine eigenständige Macht dar, welche über die Einhaltung der Gesetze wacht.

Idealtypischer Weise besteht die Exekutive aus dem Fürsten, Monarchen bzw. der Obrigkeit. Der Senat oder eine andere Gruppe stellen die Legislative. Schließlich sind Unabhängige (Richter) für die Judikative verantwortlich. Formal ist die vollständige Gewaltenteilung zwischen Exekutive, Legislative und Judikative bei Montesquieu angelegt, allerdings besitzt die Judikative in Form der richterlichen Gewalt noch bei weitem nicht den Stellenwert, den sie heute besitzt.[42]

---

[40] Montesquieu, C.d. Vom Geist der Gesetze, S. 53
[41] Zum Folgenden vgl. Druwe, U. Politische Theorie, S. 157
[42] Beyme, K.v., Politische Theorien im Zeitalter der Ideologien, S. 77

Ausführlich rechtfertigt Montesquieu den Gedanken der Gewaltenteilung: „Wenn die Ausübung der gesetzgebenden und der vollziehenden Gewalt einer einzigen Person oder einer einzigen Behörde zusteht, so gibt es keine Freiheit, weil zu befürchten ist, dass alsdann der betreffende Alleinherrscher oder die betreffende Behörde nach Willkür Gesetze geben, die sie auch willkürlich vollziehen können. Es gibt auch keine Freiheit, wo die richterliche nicht von der gesetzgebenden und der vollziehenden getrennt ist. Wäre sie mit der gesetzgebenden vereinigt, so käme dies der Aufrichtung einer schrankenlosen Macht über Leben und Freiheit der Bürger gleich; denn der Richter könnte selbst die Gesetze aufstellen. Wäre sie mit der vollziehenden Gewalt vereinigt, so könnte der Richter seine Entscheidungen mit der Kraft des Unterdrückers durchsetzen."[43]

## 6.5 Staatsform

Als Staatsform präferiert Montesquieu als Erbe der antiken wie humanistischen Staatslehre die Monarchie, wobei die oben getroffene Einschränkung zu beachten ist. So soll ein König oder Fürst die Obrigkeit bilden, wobei das Merkmal der drei geteilten Gewalten wichtig ist. V.a. die Despotie, aber auch die Republik werden von Montesquieu weitgehend abgelehnt. Bei der Monarchie pocht Montesquieu auf die verfassungsmäßige Ordnung, welche u.a. die drei Gewalten Judikative, Legislative und Exekutive trennt. Gleichzeitig sollen die drei Gewalten

---

[43] Montesquieu, C.d., Vom Geist der Gesetze, S. 53

aber so miteinander verzahnt sein, dass sie sich gegenseitig kontrollieren. Ein wichtiges Moment bei Montesquieu ist, dass die Stimmabgabe des Volkes öffentlich erfolgen muss, während die Abstimmungen der Legislative und der Regierung geheim sein müssen.[44]

Letztlich kann man sagen, dass es Montesquieus Bestreben ist, eine geeignete Mischung von monarchischer, aristokratischer und demokratischer Herrschaft zu finden. Dieses Desiderat lässt sich für ihn am ehesten in einer konstitutionell verfassten, aufgeklärten Monarchie auf der Basis einer Gewaltenteilung zwischen Krone, Adel und Bürgertum und auf der Grundlage gegenseitiger Kontrolle der Staatsgewalten einlösen. Leitbild ist hierbei eine sowohl aristokratisch als auch demokratisch orientierte Monarchie. Montesquieu betont zudem die Notwendigkeit einer Repräsentativverfassung.

### 6.6 Kulturrelativismus

Montesquieu leitete die Einsicht, dass politische Systeme und Regierungsformen kulturrelativistisch zu interpretieren sind und nicht jedes Volk für jede Staatsform geeignet ist. So sollte der jeweils vorherrschende Menschenschlag bzw. der politische Charakter der Menschen die Staatsform prägen. Diese kulturalistisch-individualistische Interpretation der Verfassungslehre bezieht also anthropogene und historisch-kulturelle Faktoren ein und zeigt sich

---

[44] Schmidt, M.G., Demokratietheorien, S. 53

damit erstaunlich variabel. Die ideengeschichtliche Relevanz von Montesquieu für moderne Demokratien ist aufgrund des Gewaltenteilungsprinzips kaum zu überschätzen.

# 7. Rousseaus Staatstheorie

## 7.1 Biographischer und historischer Kontext

Jean-Jacques Rousseau wurde 1712 in Genf geboren und starb 1778 in der Nähe von Paris. Rousseaus Lebenswerk zeichnet sich durch Vielfältigkeit aus. So war Rousseau Komponist, Romanschriftsteller, Pädagoge und Autor einer viel beachteten Autobiographie, welche nicht zuletzt Johann Wolfgang v. Goethe zu „Dichtung und Wahrheit" inspirierte. 1743/44 erhielt Rousseau als Sekretär des französischen Botschafters Einblick in die Praxis der Diplomatie und der Staatsverwaltung.[45] Das Leben von Rousseau zeichnet sich durch einen eher unglücklichen und unsteten Verlauf aus, denn er brach mit fast allen Freunden, hatte häufig Angst vor Verfolgung und zog sich schließlich in die Einsamkeit zurück.

Rousseau gehörte den Philosophen der französischen Aufklärung an, allerdings wandte er sich in seinen Schriften gegen den von der Aufklärung gelobten Fortschritt.[46] Manchen gilt Rousseau heute als Antipode pragmatisch-liberalen Denkens[47] bzw. als Gegenspieler des liberal-repräsentativen Demokratieverständnisses.[48] Der Fortschrittsgläubigkeit und Verklärung von Naturwissenschaften und Fort-

---

[45] Schmitz, M., Rousseau, S. 756
[46] Politik und Unterricht. Zeitschrift zur Gestaltung des politischen Unterrichts, S. 7
[47] Druwe, U., Politische Theorie, S. 157
[48] Speth, R., Jean-Jaques Rousseau, S. 124

schritt zu Zeiten der Aufklärung setzte Rousseau die Unschuld des Naturzustands entgegen, welcher dem fortschreitenden Sittenzerfall entgegenwirken sollte. Für Rousseau reüssierte nach seiner Flucht aus der Vaterstadt das von einer reichen Minderheit beherrschte Genf zum Muster eines demokratischen Kleinstaats.

## 7.2 Menschenbild und Naturzustand

Rousseau betonte die Künstlichkeit der Gesellschaft. Einen Grund dafür sah er in der immerwährenden Fortentwicklung der Künste und Wissenschaften. Im „Gesellschaftsvertrag" allerdings versucht er die Transformation des Urzustandes in eine entwickelte Gesellschaft zu rechtfertigen. Die bestmöglichste Kompatibilität des Menschen an einen solchen unnatürlichen, also „staatlichen" Zustand, wo seine naturgegebene Güte leicht den gefährdenden Tatsachen einer organisierten Gesellschaft unterliegt, soll seiner Meinung nach gefunden werden. Im Gegensatz zu Hobbes und Locke findet bei Rousseau eine naiv-idealistische Verklärung des Naturzustands statt.

Die Hauptproblematik liegt bei Rousseaus Anthropologie in der Priorität des Selbsterhaltungstriebs. Im Naturzustand wirft sich unter dieser Prämisse die Frage auf, inwieweit sich der Mensch vom Tier unterscheidet. Dies wird von Rousseau mit der Behauptung beantwortet, dass es nicht so sehr das Verstehen können des Menschen, als vielmehr dessen Möglichkeit der Realisierung seiner Freiheit sei.

Diese Realisierungsmöglichkeit begründet er mit der Geistlichkeit der Seele. Der Naturzustand bei Rousseau ist ein Zustand absoluter Freiheit. Diese Freiheit kann sich folglich in einem ex post Naturzustand nur verringern.

## 7.3 Vertragsschluss und Ziel der Staatsbildung

Ein wesentliches Ziel der Staatsbildung ist die maximale Aufrechterhaltung der individuellen Freiheit. Rousseau sagt über die Entstehung des Staats: "Dieser Akt des Zusammenschlusses schafft augenblicklich anstelle der Einzelpersonen jedes Vertragspartners eine sittliche Gesamtkörperschaft, die aus ebenso vielen Gliedern besteht, wie die Versammlung Stimmen hat, und die durch ebendiesen Akt ihre Einheit, ihr gemeinschaftliches Ich, ihr Leben und ihren Willen erhält."[49] In der Staatlichkeit werden alle Rechte auf einen Souverän übertragen, welcher aber nicht partizipierendes Bestandteil des Vertrages ist. Der Mensch entwickelt sich von einem Normalzustand (Urzustand) zu einem Zustand der Moralität. Dies bedeutet, dass der Staat zum Status der Gerechtigkeit und die Basis des Rechts wird. Die natürliche Freiheit des Urzustandes wird nämlich durch die einer zivilen und moralischen Ordnung ersetzt. Andererseits gilt zum Verhältnis von Naturzustand und Staatlichkeit: "Der Mensch

---

[49] Rousseau, J.J., Vom Gesellschaftsvertrag oder Grundsätze des Staatrechts, S. 5

ist frei geboren, und überall liegt er in Ketten."[50] Die individuelle Freiheit der natürlichen Ebene des Naturzustandes kann im Staat nicht mehr realisiert werden. Individuation und Individualität erfahren im Gemeinwesen Beschränkungen durch den allgemeinen Willen, d.h. den volonté générale.

Die Ziele der Staatsbildung bei Rousseau sind der Schutz und die Freiheit des Einzelnen, die Vereinigung der gemeinsamen Kraft aller und dass die Freiheit des Einzelnen erhalten bleiben soll.

### 7.4 Organisierung des Staats

Der Souverän zur Ausübung der staatlichen Gewalt ist bei Rousseau die Exekutive. Dabei reichen die möglichen Regierungsformen von der Monarchie (ein Herrscher) und Aristokratie (mehrere herrschen) bis zur Demokratie (alle herrschen). Rousseau hält die Form der Demokratie für wenig praktikabel und präferiert die aristokratische Republik, wobei dennoch das Paradoxon gilt, dass alle herrschen und eine Identität zwischen Herrscher und Beherrschten vorhanden ist.

Nach Rousseau ist der Wille der Gemeinschaft identisch mit dem eigenen Willen des Einzelnen. Deswegen wäre bei Rousseau Theorie immanent das Repräsentationsprinzip fehl am Platz. E ist nach Rousseau die Pflicht des Einzelnen, den ganz bestimmten Willen des Individuums unter die Allge-

---

[50] Rousseau, J.J., Vom Gesellschaftsvertrag oder Grundsätze des Staatrechts, S. 97

meinheit unterzuordnen, falls dieser differieren sollte. Der *volonté générale* betrifft die gesamten Allgemeininteressen. Er ist der Ausdruck eines universellen Objekts, nämlich der des souveränen Volkes, welches die Konsequenz der Begrifflichkeiten Allgemeinwohl und Vorteile für alle nach sich zieht. Der *volonté de tous* berücksichtigt Privatsphäreninteressen und ist die Summe der unterschiedlichen, individuellen Willen. Die Menschen sind zwar von sich/Natur aus nach dem Guten bestrebt, aber nicht immer in der Lage, dieses Gute zu erkennen und definieren. Deshalb ist der volonté de tous von Anfang an eher irrelevant. Der volonté générale hingegen ist immer im Recht und bedarf keiner weiteren Legitimation. Die Güte des Naturzustands hat sich in ein neues moralisches Moment des Gesellschaftsvertrages transformiert. Der Souverän ist in der Theorie von Rousseau ausschließlich in der Lage, das Realisieren des Guten, des Allgemeinwohls im Blick zu haben.

### 7.5 Inhaber der staatlichen Gewalt

Rousseau legt also das Monopol der Frage, was gut für die Menschen ist, in die Hände des Souveräns. Mögliche Einwände wie, dass das eine Vorstufe eines totalitären Staates sein könnte, werden vermeintlich durch die Argumentation, dass der Souverän ja alle und damit alle Teil des volonté générale seien, weggewischt.

So betrachtet bedeutet der volonté générale Theorie immanent eine Aufklärung und den wirklichen

Willen des Volkes. Folglich ist für Rousseau eine Pluralität der Meinungen nicht akzeptabel. Falls sich verschiedene Fraktionen im Staate herausbilden, kann der volonté générale nicht mehr in dem von ihm selber definierten Sinne gültig sein. Es ist vom heutigen Standpunkt her gesehen durchaus schwierig, diese Überlegungen nachzuvollziehen. Noch schwieriger wird es, wenn man sich vor Augen hält, dass Rousseau feststellt, dass der volonté générale und der Gesellschaftsvertrag eigentlich diejenigen Sachen sind, die der Mensch in seiner absoluten Freiheit des Naturzustandes sucht und diese folglich zu einem gelungenen, glücklichen Leben beitragen.

Über die Legitimation und den Fortbestand der politischen Körperschaft wird gesagt, dass die Gesetze ununterbrochen neue Kraft gewinnen und der Souverän sie nicht widerruft, da er sie für gut erachtet.

Provokativ formuliert sind bei Rousseau die Staatsbürger selber identisch mit dem Staatsoberhaupt. Zugleich sind alle Untertanen.

Eine Abschaffung des Souveräns ist bei Rousseau konsequenter Weise stark relativiert, vielmehr wird ein kontinuierlicher Staat propagiert. Dies ist auch dem philosophischen System Rousseaus immanent und deshalb daraus folgernd logisch zwingend, da ja der Souverän alle sind und da der volonté générale ja nur das Gute für alle meint – auch wenn alle dies nicht so verstehen – und der volonté de tous partiell von dem erstgenannten differieren kann.

Das Volk ist bei Rousseau oberster Souverän, Staatsoberhaupt und Gesetzgeber. Diese Souveränität ist ein nicht delegierbares Recht, so dass ein parlamentarisches System mit Repräsentanten undenkbar ist. Das Volk als Souverän erlässt also beispielsweise Gesetze, welche auf dem Allgemeinwillen beruhen. Auch Theorie immanent ist an dieser Argumentationsfigur problematisch, dass keine Kriterien vorhanden sind, wie festgestellt werden kann, ob ein Gesetz auf dem Allgemeinwillen (volonté générale) und nicht etwa auf der Summe der Partikularwillen (volonté de tous) basiert. Ebenso fragwürdig sind residualkategorische Rundumschläge wie Vernunft und Moral, welche ja im Allgemeinwillen impliziert sind.

## 7.6 Staatsform

Über die in der Theorie von Rousseau vorhandene Staatsform kann man trefflich streiten. Common sense ist dabei, das es sich um eine Art der direkten Demokratie handelt, welche keine repräsentativen Elemente kennt. Man kann auch von einer Identitätstheorie der Demokratie sprechen. Es herrscht Volkssouveränität und eine Identität von Regierenden und Regierten.

## 8. Hobbes und der „Große Lauschangriff"[51]

Nicht nur der innerwissenschaftliche Begründungs-, sondern auch der außerwissenschaftliche Verwertungszusammenhang bedient sich gerne der Politischen Ideengeschichte, um Vorstellungen über die Demokratie und Politikinhalte, sogenannte Policies als konkrete Politikentscheidungen,[52] zu legitimieren und plausibilisieren. Politiker berufen sich auf Traditionen politischer Vorstellungen und evozieren somit den Eindruck, dass ihre Ausführungen wissenschaftlich abgesichert und somit legitim seien.

Problematisch ist diese Vorgehensweise immer dann, wenn die Politische Ideengeschichte von Politikern instrumentalisiert und manipuliert wird, um Ideen und Policies populär zu machen, welche dem Geist der Demokratie und dem Grundgesetz widersprechen.

Es sollen also die de facto längst erfolgten Legitimationsmöglichkeiten bzw. -grenzen des „großen Lauschangriffs", also der in Deutschland früher zu Recht kontrovers diskutierten Erweiterung der Rechte von Geheimdiensten und Vollzugsbehörden zur Belauschung privater Wohnungen, die vermutlich durch das organisierte Verbrechen bzw. deren Akteure als für Teile der Exekutive (vermeintlich) unantastbare Rückzugsräume benutzt werden,

---

[51] Zum Folgenden vgl. Schweizer, S./Schweizer, P.-J., Leviathan und Lauschangriff.
[52] Vgl. zum Begriff Policy Schweizer, S., Politische Steuerung selbstorganisierter Netzwerke, S. 24 ff.

anhand von Hobbes' Staatstheorie aufgezeigt werden.

Der „große Lauschangriff" sah vor, dass es legaler weise den Geheimdiensten und Vollzugsbehörden möglich sein soll, bei begründetem Verdacht private Wohnungen zur Verbrechensprävention und -aufklärung abzuhören, da Privatwohnungen als intimer Rückzugsraum auch zur Verbrechensplanung und -koordinierung instrumentalisiert werden. Dieses Abhören des gesprochenen Wortes in privaten Wohnungen wird unter Mithilfe technischer Geräte wie Wanzen und Richtmikrophonen geschehen.

Unter organisierter Kriminalität ist zu verstehen, dass es sich bei dieser Verbrechensform um große, effiziente Vereinigungen mit straffen hierarchischen Strukturen handelt, die formal damit unternehmensähnliche Züge aufweisen. Hauptziel der organisierten Kriminalität ist Profitmaximierung, jedoch in Größenordnungen, welche die von Unternehmungen um ein Vielfaches übersteigen.

Betätigungsfelder des organisierten Verbrechens sind insbesondere Rauschgifthandel, Menschenhandel jeglicher Couleur, Prostitution, Schutzgelderpressungen, Waffenhandel und Wirtschaftskriminalität.

Dabei weist das organisierte Verbrechen heutzutage starke Globalisierungstendenzen auf. Darunter wird verstanden, dass nationale Ebenen verlassen werden und Geld-, Kapital-, Waren- und Informationsströme keinen räumlichen Beschränkungen unterworfen werden.

Diese neuen Erscheinungsformen der organisierten Kriminalität erfordern vom deutschen Staat, diesen illegalen Herausforderungen mit neuen Strategien und Taktiken zu begegnen. Ein mögliches Instrument der Verbrechensbekämpfung ist der „große Lauschangriff".

Die Rechtmäßigkeit des „großen Lauschangriffs" wurde in der öffentlichen Diskussion kontrovers erörtert.

Aus dem Grundgesetz ließ sich dabei keine eindeutige Antwort hinsichtlich der Rechtmäßigkeit des „großen Lauschangriffs" ableiten. Dies liegt v.a. an dem Spannungsverhältnis von Art. 13 (1) GG und Art. 13 (3) GG. Art. 13 (3) GG enthält nämlich die Möglichkeit der Einschränkung von Art 13 (1) GG. Diese Einschränkung hat durch Gesetz zu erfolgen.

Es scheint auf der Hand zu liegen, dass Hobbes' Staatstheorie die Legitimität des staatlich verordneten „großen Lauschangriffs" rechtfertigt. Eine Alternative zu dieser Lösung scheint zunächst ausgeschlossen.

Bei näherer Betrachtung der Dinge kommt man aber zu dem Schluss, dass es auch eine mögliche Alternative zu der den Lauschangriff bejahenden Lösung geben kann, auch wenn diese nicht so überzeugend wirkt. Sie wird aber trotzdem dargelegt, da angedeutet werden soll, dass mit dem ersten Lösungsansatz nicht unbedingt eine unumstößliche Antwort vorliegen muss. Die Alternative besteht darin, die Legitimation des „großen Lauschangriffs" mit Zurückhaltung, ja sogar mit Ablehnung, zu betrachten. Bei dieser zweiten Lösungsalternative scheint die Kompatibilität mit Hobbes' Grundintention der politischen Theorie eher fraglich.

*Erste Lösungsvariante, Rechtfertigung des „Großen Lauschangriffs":* Der Modellmensch ist bei Hobbes mit Leidenschaften und Bedürfnissen ausgestattet. Als Gegenpol spielen die Axiome der Vernunft und Furcht eine große Rolle. Das dem homo oeconomicus eigene nutzenmaximierende Denken bildet einen weiteren Grundpfeiler des Hobbes'schen Menschenbildes. Das oberste Ziel dieses Menschen ist die Selbsterhaltung. Aus dem Menschenbild von Hobbes lässt sich ableiten, dass eine Hinwendung zur organisierten Kriminalität zunächst mit rationalem Handeln gleichzusetzen wäre, da durch sie zunächst Chancen bestehen, den für die Selbsterhaltung nicht irrelevanten Besitz zu erwerben. Man könnte eventuell Vorteile im Güterverteilungskampf durch den hohen Organisationsgrad und durch das kollektive Handeln erwerben. Gleichzeitig muss man aber auch auf die Gefahrenseite einer Hinwendung zur organisierten Kriminalität hinweisen, da z.B. durch bandeninterne und -externe Verteilungskämpfe das Leben des einzelnen Menschen stark gefährdet wird.

Die Hobbes'sche Darstellung des Naturzustandes suggeriert Ähnliches. Gleiche Menschen befinden sich wegen vorherrschender Ressourcenknappheit in einem Güterverteilungskonflikt, welcher oftmals tödlichen Ausgang haben kann. Moralische Wertung kann das Ganze nicht erfahren, da es keine allgemeinverbindliche Macht und keine für alle gleich geltenden Gesetze gibt. Da diese Situation jedoch das Primärziel der Selbsterhaltung gefährdet, betont Hobbes die Vernunftseite bzw. -komponente des Menschen und leitet daraus natürliche Gesetze ab, welche die Selbsterhaltung garantieren sollen. Da aber kein institutionalistisches Zwangssystem die Einhaltung der natürlichen Gesetze und damit das Zurückdrängen des Naturzustandes garantieren kann, muss ein Staat gegründet werden.

Bis zu diesem Punkt wird ersichtlich, dass aus dem Modell von Hobbes eine große Furcht vor etwas der organisierten Kriminalität Vergleichbarem und irregulären Vereinigungen herrscht. Eventuell lässt sich eine abstrakte Parallele zwischen dem von Hobbes gefürchteten Bürgerkrieg und der organisierten Kriminalität ziehen. Beides impliziert (zumeist materielle) Verteilungskämpfe. Die Furcht lässt sich damit begründen, dass die organisierte Kriminalität hohe Gewinne auf Kosten anderer macht. Diese Kosten können so hoch sein, dass sie massiv die Selbsterhaltungsinteressen von Individuen tangieren.

Hobbes' Lösung dieses Dilemmas besteht darin, dass jeder mit jedem einen Vertrag abschließt, um einen künstlichen Staat zu schaffen. Dieser Vertrag ist sowohl ein Entäußerungs- als auch ein Unterwerfungsvertrag. Der Souverän ist kein Vertragsmitglied, und Rechte sind gegen ihn nicht einklagbar.

Aus diesem Vertragsgedanken lässt sich eine eindeutige Rechtfertigung des „großen Lauschangriffs" ableiten. Rechte werden entäußert, und Menschen unterwerfen sich einem Souverän, der selber kein Vertragsmitglied ist und somit kein Unrecht gegen seine Untertanen ausüben kann.

Die Ausgestaltung dieses Staatswesens bleibt zunächst offen, obwohl Hobbes die Form einer Monarchie favorisiert hat. In jedem Fall besitzt der Souverän bei Hobbes eine uneingeschränkte Machtfülle, welche natürlich demokratischen Vorstellungen zuwider läuft. Eine Gewaltenteilung ist nicht existent, der Souverän vereinigt Legislative, Exekutive und Judikative in sich. Alleine der Souverän bestimmt die Mittel, mit denen Frieden und Schutz im Staat hergestellt werden können. Ferner bestimmt der Souverän Meinungen und Lehren sowie Eigentumsverteilung und Steuern.

Es wird klar ersichtlich, dass der „große Lauschangriff" aus dieser Staatsdefinition heraus per se gar keiner Legitimation bedürfte. Die Machtbefugnisse des Souveräns unterliegen gar keinen Restriktionen.

Es ist allerdings zu beachten, dass die Funktionalität der Staatsgründung erhalten bleiben soll. Das bedeutet, dass der Schutz zur Selbsterhaltung nicht unterlaufen werden darf. Das scheint beim „großen Lauschangriff" mitnichten der Fall zu sein, denn durch die Bekämpfung der organisierten Kriminalität werden die Bürger und ihr Leben geschützt.

Bürgerliche Freiheiten gibt es in dem Hobbes'schen Modell nur da, wo es keine gesetzlichen Reglementierungen gibt. Das bedeutet, dass die bürgerlichen Gesetze bürgerliche Freiheit determinieren. Neue gesetzliche Reglementierungen können von dem Souverän ohne „wenn und aber" erlassen werden. Die Untertanen haben in Hobbes' Staat keinerlei Möglichkeit gegen die Gesetze vorzugehen oder sie zu ändern.

Auch aus diesem Abschnitt ergibt sich eine problemlose Rechtfertigung des „großen Lauschangriffs". Wo Gesetze ohne Kontrollzwang erlassen werden können, keiner gegen sie vorgehen kann und Gesetze dazu bestimmt sind, bürgerliche Freiheiten zu definieren, da ist jedes neue Gesetz insoweit legitim, als es die Selbsterhaltung der Bürger garantiert.

Hobbes sah in illegalen und irregulären Vereinigungen ein großes Gefahrenpotential für den Staat. Diese Sichtweise wurde mit Kompetenzstreitigkeiten mit dem Staat und Gefahrenpotentialen für den Staat begründet. Mit aller Entschiedenheit sollte gegen diese den Staat bedrohenden Vereinigungen vorgegangen werden.

Da es sich bei der organisierten Kriminalität um Vereinigungen mit hoher struktureller Organisationskraft handelt, wären diese von Hobbes als für den Staat besonders gefährlich eingestuft worden. Da das Ziel des Staates die Gewährleistung der Selbsterhaltung von Individuen ist, lässt sich folgern, dass eine Bedrohung des Staates immer auch eine Bedrohung seiner Untertanen impliziert. Auch aus diesen Überlegungen lässt sich die Einführung des „großen Lauschangriffs" ohne weiteres rechtfertigen.

Insgesamt wurde deutlich, dass nach diesem Lösungsvorschlag der „große Lauschangriff" in allen Punkten ohne Bedenken oder Gegenargumente durch Hobbes' Vertrags- und Staatstheorie gerechtfertigt werden kann.

*Alternativlösung:* Bei der Alternativlösung muss die Akzentuierung v.a. auf der Komponente des Wohnraums liegen. Diese Betonung der Wichtigkeit der Unverletzlichkeit des Wohnraums entspricht natürlich nicht so sehr den zeitgenössischen Tendenzen von Thomas Hobbes als eher einer postmaterialistischen Sichtweise oder Lesart.

Nach dieser modernen postmaterialistischen Auffassung kann man behaupten, dass die Unverletzlichkeit des Wohnraums ein Grundrecht darstellt, welches für die individuelle Selbstverwirklichung unabdingbar ist. Man kann darüber hinaus von einer anthropologischen Grundkonstante sprechen, die bei allen Kulturen bzw. Kulturkreisen anzutreffen ist: „Unabhängig von Wohnform und Hauskonstruktion gilt in allen Kulturen, dass man den privaten Bereich ohne Einladung nicht betritt."[53]

Durch den „großen Lauschangriff" wird aber eine Wohnung sozusagen im akustischen Bereich ohne vorherige Einladung betreten. Schlimmer noch, welche die Wohnung Benutzenden wissen gar

---

[53] Grammer, K., My home is my castle, S. 16.

nicht, dass jemand ihre Wohnung „betreten" hat. Sie fühlen sich also in ihrer Intimsphäre der Unverletzbarkeit der Wohnung geborgen wie eh und je.

Außerdem können sich aus den bei dem „großen Lauschangriff" gewonnen akustischen Informationen durchaus dann bei den Belauschenden „visualisierte, optische" Handlungsabläufe in Form von assoziativen Vorstellungen zu dem gehörten Wort ergeben. Insgesamt ist die Intimsphäre des privaten Wohnraums durch den „großen Lauschangriff" immens diskreditiert. Man stelle sich nur einmal vor, dass die Wohnung eines verdächtigen Pärchens abgehört wird. Aus ermittlungstaktischen Gründen werden die Richtmikrophone und Wanzen sicherlich nicht bei intimen Handlungen und Gesprächen der beiden abgestellt, da ja jederzeit wieder Kommunikation hinsichtlich organisierter Kriminalität stattfinden kann. Gerade in diesem Punkt ist auch mit der Neugier der Belauschenden zu rechnen.

Wenn man konstatiert, dass in Zeiten, in denen die materielle Grundversorgung der Bevölkerung weitestgehend sichergestellt ist, die Selbsterhaltung in mehr als nur dem nackten Überleben besteht, dann kann man folgern, dass zwischen Selbsterhaltung und Selbstverwirklichung ein enger Zusammenhang besteht. Gerade die Selbsterhaltung ist es ja, die Thomas Hobbes durch eine Staatsgründung gesichert sehen will. Die Verletzung des Wohnraums würde dann also dem Primärzweck der Selbsterhaltung zuwiderlaufen. Hier muss eine genaue Abwägung zwischen individuellen Partikularinteressen (der Unverletzlichkeit des Wohnraums als Mitvoraussetzung der Selbsterhaltungsgarantie) und allgemeinen Interessen (Vernichtung oder Schädigung anderer Individuen durch organisierte Kriminalität) stattfinden.

Ein weiterer Faktor, welcher gegen die Rechtfertigung des „großen Lauschangriffs" sprechen kann, ist das Spannungsverhältnis zwischen Art 13 (1) GG und Art 13 (3) GG. Der Art. 13 (1) GG steht im engen Zusammenhang mit der Persönlichkeitsentfaltung, der Privatsphäre des Bürgers, und sein Sinn ist die Wahrung räumlicher Integrität und damit „der Schutz eines räumlichen Bezirks, in dem der einzelne ungestört unbeobachtet tun und lassen darf, was ihm beliebt".[54] Wieder kann man das Recht auf freie Persönlichkeitsentfaltung in engen Zusammenhang mit der von Hobbes postulierten Selbsterhaltung setzen. Verstärkt wird dieser Argumentationsstrang dadurch, dass der Unverletzlichkeit der Wohnung ein Abwehranspruch gegen den Staat innewohnt.[55] Allerdings sieht das Grundgesetz auch Einschränkungsmöglichkeiten des Art. 13 (1) GG durch den Art. 13 (3) GG vor. Die obige Argumentation wird durch die Betrachtung des Art. 13 (3) GG nicht hinfällig, da ihm eine differenzierte Auslegung zugrunde liegt.[56] Das bedeutet, dass der relativ weit gefasste Begriff der Wohnung am meisten dort greift, wo sie auch als solche hauptsächlich benutzt wird (also nicht als Arbeits-, Lagerungsstätte, Büroraum etc.). Bei der vorgegebenen Aufgabenstellung und dem

---

[54] Katz, A, Staatsrecht, S. 371.
[55] Katz, A., Staatsrecht, S. 371.
[56] Katz, A., Staatsrecht, S. 372.

damit verbundenen „großen Lauschangriff" handelt es sich aber um Privatwohnungen, welchen dann der Abwehrbereich des Art. 13 (1) GG implizit ist.

Aus den vorgenannten Begründungen lässt sich der „große Lauschangriff" durch Hobbes' Vertrags- und Staatstheorie kaum legitimieren.

*Abwägung der Lösungsvorschläge:* Es ist deutlich geworden, dass der erste Lösungsvorschlag plausibler und stringenter wirkt. Die erste Lösung ist hinsichtlich Hobbes' Vertrags- und Staatstheorie konsistenter. Sie ist sicherlich damit zu rechtfertigen, dass sie insgesamt wohl auch den Vorstellungen von Hobbes nahe kommt.

Beim zweiten Lösungsvorschlag handelt es sich um eine Lösungsinterpretation, in der auch moderne Sichtweisen und Faktoren berücksichtigt sind. Diese Variante ist nur durch die zugegebenermaßen neuzeitliche Auffassung der sehr stark abstrahierten Gleichstellung von Selbsterhaltung mit Selbstverwirklichung zu verstehen.

Aus Gründen der Konsistenz wirkt der erste Vorschlag gerechtfertigt. Dies bedeutet aber nicht, dass ihm daher der Vorzug vor der modernen Sichtweise zu geben ist. Dafür wäre eine weitere Auseinandersetzung oder Begriffsgeschichte des Privaten und Intimen vonnöten..

*Abschlussüberlegungen:* Es dürfte deutlich geworden sein, welche Gefahren von einer Instrumentalisierung und Manipulation politischer Ideengeschichte zur Legitimierung und Plausibilisierung von Policies ausgeht, welche grundlegenden demokratischen Werten, wie der Unverletzlichkeit der Privatwohnung, fundamental widersprechen. Im Falle von Hobbes liegt die Ausgangsproblematik darin begründet, dass dessen Politische Theorie demokratischen Grundsätzen zutiefst widerspricht und somit eine Anwendung derselben auf die freiheitlich-demokratische Grundordnung der Bundesrepublik nicht möglich ist.

Verliert man diese Grundprämisse allerdings einmal aus den Augen, so könnte man leicht der Gefahr erliegen, der skizzierten „Theorie immanenten" Diskussion zu folgen, zumal der Anspruch der Wissenschaftlichkeit gegeben zu sein scheint. In der wissenschaftlichen Nutzbarmachung politischer Ideengeschichte für moderne Sachverhalte kann also ein großes Gefahren- und Manipulationspotential verborgen liegen. Politiker können so, vermeintlich durch die Wissenschaftlichkeit geschützt und die Autorität der politisch-philosophischen Denker der Vorzeit abgesichert, Weltanschauungen und ideologische Tendenzen bei bestimmten Policies transportieren, welche dem demokratischen Freiheitssinn und der Unveräußerlichkeit der Privatsphäre widersprechen.

Beim vorliegenden Beispiel des großen Lauschangriffs müssten also, damit Politiker legitim im demokratischen, bundesdeutschen Rahmen argumentieren könnten, andere Ideengeschichtler herangezogen werden. Ein passenderes Beispiel wäre John Locke, welcher auch ein Kontraktualist ist und mit seiner Konnotation des Individualismus und Privaten eindeutig zu einer Negierung des großen

Lauschangriffs käme. Noch einschlägiger für moderne Demokratien wäre die Rückbesinnung auf moderne Demokratietheoretiker und Staatsvertragstheoretiker wie John Rawls. Auch hier wird die Frage des großen Lauschangriffs abschlägig beschieden und die Unverletzlichkeit der Privatsphäre in den Mittelpunkt Argumentation gestellt.

## 9. Anwendungsbeispiel Hobbes und Locke: Fallbeispiel Speichelprobe

Wurde im vorigen Kapitel untersucht, ob und wie sich umstrittene Policies wie der „Große Lauschangriff" durch Hobbes' Staatstheorie heute legitimieren lassen, so soll im Folgenden noch ein Vergleich zweier Staats- und Vertragstheoretiker hinsichtlich einer Policy untersucht werden. Die beiden Theoretiker sind Hobbes und Locke und die Policy bzw. das Anwendungsbeispiel die Legitimität von Massenspeichelproben in der männlichen Bevölkerung nach gravierenden Kapitalverbrechen.

Im Einleitungskapitel wurde gesagt, dass moderne Policies durch den Rekurs auf Staats- und Vertragstheoretiker legitimiert werden können. Konkret bedeutet das, dass Politiker/innen durch die Berufung auf Vertrags- und Staatstheoretiker eine bestimmte Policy legitimieren und der Entscheidung dafür Authentizität verschaffen wollen. Ein solches Beispiel wird im Folgenden an Hobbes und Locke an der Einführung von Massenspeichelproben nach schweren kriminellen Straftaten (damals durchzusetzende Policy) durchgespielt.[57]

*Problem:* Innerhalb der letzten Jahre geschahen verhältnismäßig viele Morde an Kindern im Alter zwischen 5 und 15 Jahren. Diesen Kapitalverbrechen geschahen oftmals aus sexuellen Tatmotiven. Die Kinder wurden in vielen Fällen zur Tatvertu-

---

[57] Zum Folgenden vergleiche Stefan Schweizer/Pia-Johanna Schweizer, Hobbes und Locke. Fallbeispiel Speichelprobe.

schung ermordet, um eine Täteridentifikation unmöglich zu machen. Vornehmlich durch die Medien wurde das Täterprofil eines äußerst gefährlichen, psychisch Kranken mit pädophilen Neigungen verbreitet. Sowohl die sexuellen Übergriffe gegen Kinder als auch deren Ermordung stellen im Bevölkerungsbewusstsein ein Sicherheitsproblem dar. Dies insbesondere, weil in der Bevölkerung Verbrechen Erwachsener gegen Kinder als besonders schlimm und bedrohlich empfunden werden.

*Politisches Problem:* Da aus der skizzierten Bedrohungslage schnell massiver Bevölkerungsunmut entstehen kann, droht dem politischen System (v.a. der Regierung) potentiell starker Unterstützungsverlust. Um diesen abwenden zu können, wird das Ausgangs- zum genuin politischen Problem. Im politischen Kontext firmiert das Thema im weiteren Sinne unter dem Etikett der Sicherheit. Engt man es weiter ein, so wird daraus der Problembereich „Innere Sicherheit". Öffentlichkeitswirksam politisch diskutiert wird das unter Slogans wie „Schützt unsere Kinder", „Lebenslang für Sextäter" und „Kastration für Pädophile". Ein weiterer politisch gewünschter Ansatzpunkt - der seinerseits systemstabilisierend wirken soll - ist die schnelle Aufklärung der Straftaten. Davon verspricht man sich einmal einkehrende Ruhe in der Bevölkerung und zum anderen präventive Auswirkungen. Eine Maßnahme, die zu dieser schnellen Tataufklärung führen soll, besteht in der Durchführung von Massenspeichelproben. Diese werden häufig aufgrund regionaler Zugehörigkeit - d.h. v.a. in dem regional angrenzenden Raum des Verbrechens - vorgenommen. Letztliches Ziel ist, den Täter durch ein positives Testergebnis - d.h. die Übereinstimmung seiner DNA mit bei dem Opfer gefundenen DNA-Spuren - identifizieren und überführen zu können. Diese Speichelproben finden zunächst auf freiwilliger Basis statt. Man erhofft sich insbesondere in kleinen Gemeinden, dass der Täter psychologisch derart stark unter Druck gerät, dass auch er sich einem Test stellt und dabei entlarvt werden kann. Bei einer solchen Vorgehensweise stellt sich die Frage, inwieweit sie legitim ist. Immerhin werden Hunderte von Männern als potentielle Verdächtige avisiert und - letztlich unschuldigerweise - angehalten und zur Speichelprobe zu kommen.

*Reformulierung als politikwissenschaftliches Problem:* Die Frage, die sich aus politikwissenschaftlicher Perspektive stellt, ist vornehmlich die der Legitimität solcher Maßnahmen. Wird im juristischen Diskurs besonders nach der Rechtmäßigkeit bzw. Legalität solcher Vorgehensweisen gefragt, so hier deshalb nach der Legitimität, weil sich die Frage aufwirft, ob und inwieweit sie unserem Demokratieverständnis und dem darin implizierten Verhältnis von Bürger und Staat entsprechen. Drastischer gewendet: Tendieren diese Maßnahmen nicht in Richtung eines (totalitären) Polizeistaats? Die aus diesem Kontext resultierende Forschungsfrage lautet: Sind die polizeilichen Maßnahmen der Massenspeichelproben legitim bzw. gerechtfertigt? In unserem Fall muss man diese Frage auf den Rechtsanwalt im Fall Tobias übertragen: Ist das massive polizeiliche Drängen auf eine Speichelprobe des Rechtsanwalts legitim? Über die Beantwortung dieser Frage kann man geteilter Meinung sein. Um Äußerungen zu diesem Sachverhalt fundieren und ihrerseits legitimieren zu können, bedient man sich beispielsweise der politischen Ideengeschichte. Philosophische Konzepte der Vergangenheit werden herangezogen, um anvisierte Meinungen plausibilisieren und legitimieren zu können. Die dafür anzuwendende Methode ist die der rationalen Rekonstruktion.

*Alltagsperspektivische Abgrenzung und Problemspezifizierung:* Diskutiert wurde die Methode der Massenspeichelproben zum ersten Mal ernsthaft vor etlichen Jahren nach dem Mordfall J. Nitsch. Damals allerdings wurde die Freiwilligkeit der Testung als zentrales Kriterium hervorgehoben. Dadurch konnte man u.a. durch Ausschlussverfahren bestimmen, wer als Täter nicht in Betracht kam. Die Testmethode wurde gängige Praxis und männliche Bevölkerungsteile ganzer Landstriche wurden vornehmlich nach sexuellen und Kapitalverbrechen gegen Kinder zu Speichelproben aufgerufen. Inzwischen hat sich die Testungspraxis und das bis dato damit verbundene Primat der Freiwilligkeit beinahe in sein Gegenteil verkehrt. Im Fall des ermordeten Tobias bei Weil im Schönbuch rief die Polizei regional (da der Täter wohl Ortskenntnisse besitzen musste) die männliche Bevölkerung zum Speicheltest auf. Der Täter konnte durch diese Tests bisher nicht identifiziert werden. Ein Rechtsanwalt verweigerte die Probe. Dies - wie zu lesen war - wohl auch deshalb, weil er ein „Beinahe-Alibi" vorweisen konnte. Die Polizei ihrerseits gab sich mit dem „Nein" des Rechtsanwalts nicht zufrieden. Ohne jeglichen stichhaltigen Grund seitens der Polizei und Staatsanwaltschaft wurde sogar offiziell über eine Täterschaft des Rechtsanwalts gemutmaßt. Dies scheint bei einer nüchtern-objektiven Betrachtung der Falldaten wenig wahrscheinlich. Implikationen sind die folgenden: Es werden fundamentale demokratische Rechtsstaatsprinzipien (insbesondere des Straf- und Strafprozessrechts) verletzt. Aus heutiger ideenpluralistisch geschulter Sicht scheint es eine Abwägungsfrage zu sein, ob Sicherheitsinteressen oder die Rechte des Einzelnen Vorrang genießen sollten. Diese Frage kann man unter Zuhilfenahme von politischen Konzepten der Ideengeschichte unterschiedlich beantworten.

*Problembezogene Ausrichtung des Modellzusammenhangs, empirisches Relativ und Problemlösung Hobbes:* Aus dem Gesagten ergibt sich in aller Kürze folgende Problemlösung: Menschen, die junge Kinder sexuell missbrauchen und umbringen (oder umgekehrt) stellen eine große Gefahr für die Gemeinschaft dar. Der Rechtsanwalt ist aufgrund regionaler Ansässigkeit und einem nicht zweifelsfreien Alibi ein potentiell Verdächtiger. Unabdingbare Prämisse, den Herrschaftsvertrag einzugehen, ist, dass das zu schaffende Staatsgebilde die Selbsterhaltung des Einzelnen im Inneren wie Äußeren erhalten kann. Genau diese Selbsterhaltung ist der Staat aber bei den getöteten Kindern – in unserem Fall Tobias – nicht zu garantieren imstande. Kann der Staat seinen protektiven Funktionen hinsichtlich der Bürger nicht mehr nachkommen, ist er aufgrund des dann in Kraft tretenden Widerstandsrechts in seinen Grundfesten gefährdet. Es ist also mehr als staatliche Pflicht – nämlich ureigenstes Bestandsinteresse und eigentliche Grundfunktion – krasse Rechtsverstöße zur Abwehr potentiellen Schadens von den Bürgern zu ahnden. Ein polizeilicher Aufruf zur Speichelprobe entspricht also sowohl staatlichem als auch bürgerlichem Funktions- und Selbsterhaltungsinteresse. So ist es also zulässig, geeignet und legitim, den Rechtsanwalt zur Speichelprobe aufzurufen und bei Ablehnung – wie geschildert – so unter Druck zu setzen, dass er eventuell doch dem Aufruf nachkommt. Antizipierter Weise könnten durch diese prinzipielle Vorgehensweise die staatliche Rechtsordnung wiederhergestellt und der innere Friede gesichert werden.

*Problembezogene Ausrichtung des Modellzusammenhangs, empirisches Relativ und Problemlösung Locke:* Bei Locke liegt die Akzentuierung stärker auf Individualismus und Freiheit und nicht mehr nur auf Selbsterhaltung. Vielmehr machen die ersten beiden Aspekte einen großen Teil der Selbsterhaltung aus. Demnach wäre im Fall Tobias nicht so sehr die Abwehr von Bedrohungen, sondern eher die staatlich garantierten, individuellen Freiheitsrechte zu fokussieren. Locke hebt eben die staatliche Pflicht zur Wahrung individueller Rechte besonders hervor. Allerdings ist – modellimmanent – zwischen dem Naturrecht, in dem das Recht auf Wahrung der persönlichen Integrität besteht, und dem (staatlich garantierten) positiven Recht, in dem die Beweislast beim Staat liegt und die Unschuldsvermutung bis zur Verurteilung gilt, zu differenzieren Die implizierte mittelbare Zwangsanwendung auf den sich der Speichelprobe verweigernden Rechtsanwalt ist also nicht legitim. Hier sogar im gesteigerten Maße, da der mittelbare Druck – wie oben geschildert – ziemlich unmittelbar wird, denn die Polizei spricht nur aufgrund der Speicheltestverweigerung von Tatverdacht und ähnlichem. Diese Beweisumkehr und Schuldvermutung impliziert eine massive Beschädigung der persönlichen Integrität und ist somit weder zulässig noch legitim. Das tatsächliche Vorgehen der Polizei im Falle des Rechtsanwalts wäre also illegitim und würde sogar den Staatszweck und die Staatsfunktion konterkarieren. Man könnte gegebenenfalls sogar von Machtmissbrauch und Amtsanmaßung ausgehen, was wiederum die Frage nach dem Widerstandsrecht aufwirft.

*Problemlösung und Fazit:* Bei der Gesamtfallbetrachtung müssen zunächst zwei moderne straf- und strafprozessrechtliche Aspekte bedacht werden: Niemand muss seine Unschuld, sondern die Staatsgewalt die Schuld beweisen und bis zur Verurteilung gilt die Unschuldsvermutung. Beide Aspekte werden im Sachverhalt Tobias aufs Gröbste verletzt. Nach Hobbes zielt die von der Polizei angeordnete Maßnahme auf die Wiederherstellung der staatlichen Rechtsordnung und die Sicherung des innergesellschaftlichen Friedens. Es ist die unabdingbare Pflicht des Staates, alle geeigneten Maßnahmen zu ergreifen, die erforderlich sind, um aktuelle Ordnungsverstöße zu ahnden und potentiellen Schaden von den Bürgern abzuwenden. Der an den Rechtsanwalt ergehende Aufruf zur Abgabe einer Speichelprobe ist demnach legitim. Nach Locke hingegen sind staatliche Maßnahmen illegitim, wenn dadurch individuelle Rechte verletzt werden, zum Naturrecht gehört der Anspruch auf Wahrung der persönlichen Integrität, zum Gesetzesrecht der Anspruch auf Einhaltung der von der Legislative erlassenen Normen. Die in früheren vergleichbaren Fällen mittelbare und im Fall Tobias doch schon beinahe als unmittelbar zu bezeichnende Gewalt, die durch den massiven Aufruf zur freiwilligen Abgabe einer Speichelprobe auf Verweigerer ausgelöst wird, beschädigt zum einen die persönliche Integrität (Naturrecht) und verstößt zum anderen gegen das Strafverfolgungsrecht (Gesetzesrecht). Der Aufruf ist demnach im Sinne Lockes illegitim, im Sinne Hobbes' mehr oder weniger problemlos legitimierbar und entspricht dem Staatzweck und -interesse. **Fazit:** Berechtigung und Plausibilität beider Argumentationsgänge entspricht einer werte- und ideenpluralistisch ausgerichteten Gesellschaft.

# Literatur

**Ballestrem, K. G.**, Vertragspolitische Ansätze in der politischen Philosophie, in: Zeitschrift für Politik, 30 Jg. (1983), S. 1-17

**Beyme, K.v.**, Politische Theorien im Zeitalter der Ideologien. 1789-1945. Westdeutscher Verlag. Wiesbaden 2002

**Copleston, F.**, A history of Philosophy, Volume V, Part I, Image Books Edition 1964

**Dießelhorst, M.**, Nachwort. In: T. Hobbes, Leviathan, Philipp Reclam jun. GmbH & Co., Stuttgart 1970, S. 307-323

**Druwe, U.**, Studienführer Politikwissenschaft, Neuried, 1994

**Druwe, U.**, Politische Theorie, 2. Auflage, Ars una, Neuried, 1995

**Euchner, W.**, Thomas Hobbes, in: Münkler, H., Fetscher, I. (Hrsg.): Pipers Handbuch Politischer Ideen, Bd. 3, München 1985, S. 353-368

**Forsyth, M.**, Hobbes's contractarianism. In: Boucher, D., Kelly, P. (Hrsg.): The social contract from Hobbes to Rawls, New York 1994

**Gies, H.**, Geschichtsunterricht. Ein Handbuch zur Unterrichtsplanung. Köln 2004

**Grammer, K.**, My home is my castle. Behausung, Wohnen und urbanes Leben. In: Funkkolleg: Der Mensch. Anthropologie heute. Tübingen: Deutsches Institut für Fernstudien an der Universität Tübingen 1993, S. 10-23

**Grammes, T.**, Exemplarisches lernen. In: Sander, W. (Hrsg.), Handbuch politische Bildung. Praxis und Wissenschaft.Schwalbach/Ts. 1997, S. 49-62

**Grosser, D.**, Lehrziele und Prinzipien der Stoffauswahl in der politischen Bildung. In:

Grosser, D. (Hrsg.), Politischer Unterricht. Fachwissenschaftliche und didaktische Analysen. Mit Unterrichtsskizzen. Freiburg im Breisgau 1976, S. 9-24

**Günther-Arndt, H.**, Historisches Lernen und Wissenserwerb. In: Günther-Arndt, H. (Hrsg.), Geschichtsdidaktik. Praxishandbuch für die Sekundarstufe I und II. Berlin 2005, S. 23-47

**Hausmann, F.-R.**, Montesquieu, in: Metzler Philosophen Lexikon, zweite aktualisierte und erweiterte Auflage, Stuttgart 1995, S. 605-607

**Hobbes, T.**, Leviathan. Stuttgart 1996

**Kaiser, G.**, Aufklärung, Empfindsamkeit, Sturm und Drang. 25. Auflage. Tübingen 1996

**Katz, A.**, Staatsrecht. Heidelberg 1994

**Kersting, W.**, Thomas Hobbes zur Einführung, Hamburg 1992

**W. Kersting**, Die politische Philosophie des Gesellschaftsvertrags. Darmstadt 1994

**Luhmann, N.**, Die Gesellschaft der Gesellschaft. Band 2. Frankfurt am Main 1997

**Luhmann, N.,** Das Erziehungssystem der Gesellschaft. Herausgegeben von Dieter Lenzen. Frankfurt am Main 2002

**Massing, P./Breit, G.,** Vorwort. In: Massing, P./Breit, G. (Hrsg.), Demokratie-Theorien. Von der Antike bis zur Gegenwart. Bonn 2003, S. 7-10

**Massing, P.,** Demokratie-Lernen oder Politik-Lernen. In: Breit, G./Schiele, S. (Hrsg.), Demokratie-Lernen als Aufgabe der politischen Bildung. Bonn 2002, S. 160-187

**Meyer-Drawe, K.,** Kulturwissenschaftliche Pädagogik, in: Jaeger, F./Straub, J. (Hrsg.): Handbuch der Kulturwissenschaften. Paradigmen und Disziplinen. Band 2., Stuttgart 2004, S. 602-614

**Montesquieu, C.d.,** Vom Geist der Gesetze, in: Kochendörfer, J. (Hrsg.), Geschichte Geschehen. Berufliche Oberstufe. Leipzig 2003, S. 53

**Pesch, V.,** Charles de Montesquieu, in: Massing, P., Breit, G. (Hrsg.), Demokratie-Theorien, Bonn, 2003, S. 109-117

**Politik und Unterricht.** Zeitschrift zur Gestaltung des politischen Unterrichts. Staatstheorien. Sonderheft 1984. 10. Jahrgang

**Reinhardt, S.,** Politikdidaktik. Praxishandbuch für die Sekundarstufe I und II. Berlin 2005

**Rousseau, J.J.,** Vom Gesellschaftsvertrag oder Grundsätze des Staatrechts. Reclam. Stuttgart. 1991

**Sauer, M.**, Geschichte unterrichten. Eine Einführung in die Didaktik und Methodik. Seelze 2001

**Schiele, S.**, Politische Bildung neu vermessen? In: Breit, G./Schiele, S. (Hrsg.), Demokratie-Lernen als Aufgabe der politischen Bildung. Bonn 2002, S. 1-12

**Schmidt, M.G.**, Demokratietheorien. Eine Einführung. 2. Auflage. Leske + Budrich. Opladen 1997

**Schmidt, S.**, Die Selbstorganisation des Sozialsystems Literatur im 18. Jahrhundert. Frankfurt am Main 1989

**Schmitz, M.**, Rousseau, in: Metzler Philosophen Lexikon, zweite aktualisierte und erweiterte Auflage, Stuttgart 1995, S. 755-761

**Schneider, T.**, John Locke, in: Metzler Philosophen Lexikon, zweite aktualisierte und erweiterte Auflage, Stuttgart 1995, S. 512-517

**Schottky, R.**, Untersuchungen zur Geschichte der staatsphilosophischen Vertragstheorie im 17. und 18. Jahrhundert, Amsterdam-Atlanta 1995

**Schweizer, S.**, Politische Steuerung selbstorganisierter Netzwerke. Baden-Baden 2003

**Schweizer, S./Schweizer, P.-J.**, Leviathan und Lauschangriff, in: sic et non. Zeitschrift für Philosophie und Kultur. Im netz. #8/2007, S. 1-37 (URL: http://sicetnon.org/Leviathan_und_Lauschangriff_Schweizer.pdf)

**Schweizer, S./Schweizer, P.J.**, Hobbes und Locke. Fallbeispiel Speichelprobe. München 2008

**Seliger, M.**, John Locke, in: Münkler, H., Fetscher, I (Hrsg.): Pipers Handbuch politischer Ideen, Bd. 3, München, 1985, S. 381-400

**Siep, L.**, Vertragstheorie - Ermächtigung und Kritik von Herrschaft?, in: Bermbach, U., Kodalle, K.-M. (Hrsg): Furcht und Freiheit. Leviathan Diskussion 300 Jahre nach Thomas Hobbes, Opladen 1982, S. 129-145

**Speth,, R.**, Thomas Hobbes, in: Massing, P., Breit, G. (Hrsg.), Demokratie-Theorien, Bonn, 2003, S. 94-98

**Speth,, R.**, John Locke, in: Massing, P., Breit, G. (Hrsg.), Demokratie-Theorien, Bonn, 2003, S. 99-108

**Speth,, R.**, Jean-Jaques Rousseau, in: Massing, P., Breit, G. (Hrsg.), Demokratie-Theorien, Bonn, 2003, S. 118-124

**Stegmüller, W.**, Aufsätze zu Kant und Wittgenstein, Darmstadt 1970

**Sutor, B.**, Didaktik des politischen Unterrichts. Paderborn 1971

**Sutor, B.**, Geschichte als politische Bildung. In: Mickel, W. (Hrsg.) Politikunterricht. Im Zusammenhang mit seinen Nachbarfächern. München 1979, S. 82-102

**Waldron, J.**, John Locke, in: Boucher, D., Kelly, P. (Hrsg.): The social contract from Hobbes to Rawls, New York 1994